Vasquez

California's Forgotten Bandit

By Jack Jones

Akira Press
Carlsbad, Calif.

Vasquez
California's Forgotten Bandit
By Jack Jones

Published by ***Akira Press***
2604-B El Camino Real
Carlsbad, CA 92008
Box 143

As this book is an exploration of how the bandit Tiburcio Vasquez was portrayed by the various writers of his time and since, the author cannot vouch for the veracity of all those biographers' assertions, many of which were clearly romanticized fiction.

Library of Congress Catalog Card Number: 96-95147

ISBN 0-9653770-0-8

Cover layout by Jim O'Meara, Carlsbad Graphics
Painting of Vasquez by the author

Vasquez at age 40

--Courtesy California State Library
California Collection

History, n. An account mostly false, of events mostly unimportant, which are brought about by rulers, mostly knaves, and soldiers, mostly fools.

--Ambrose Bierce, *The Devil's Dictionary*

CONTENTS

Foreword

Tiburcio Vasquez, who terrorized California during its first quarter century of statehood, was never as famous east of the Sierra Madre as the legendary Joaquin Murrieta. While Murrieta appears to have been a partly fictional figure who grew out of the exploits of at least five Mexican bandits, Vasquez was no myth. He was viewed as a hero by many native Californians who had seen the *yanquis* sweep in the moment gold was discovered. Vasquez professed to have wanted to lead a revolt against the *Americano* "invaders." After he was finally seized in 1874 at Greek George's adobe house near what is now the intersection of Laurel Canyon and Hollywood Boulevards in Hollywood, he told the editor of *The Los Angeles Daily Herald*, "Given $60,000, I would be able to recruit enough arms and men to revolutionize Southern California."

Considering that Tiburcio Vasquez was known to have killed only two men during his 20-year career, it is remarkable that he achieved the notoriety he did as he and his band rode down out of the canyons to prey on stagecoaches, lone riders, ranchos and remote Americano businesses. He was decently educated, came from a respectable family and was gentlemanly in his own way.

As for Joaquin Murrieta, it has been pointed out that not a single photograph of him exists, while Vasquez willingly posed for the camera on the very eve of his hanging. Robert Greenwood, in his 1974 book on the life of Vasquez, noted that there was never a solid description of Murrieta, even though he became the most famous western outlaw with the exception of Billy the Kid. Joaquin was pretty much the creation of John Rollin Ridge, a Cherokee who called himself "Yellowbird" and was the author of *Life and Adventures of Joaquin Murieta*, published in 1854.* According to Greenwood:

> ...there is serious question and doubt about the exploits attributed to this person: indeed, even as to his identity and fate. There could have been a Joaquin Murrieta (a minor cattle thief in the Mother Lode country of California) but certainly not a Joaquin Murrieta such as Ridge described. It is more likely that there were five bandits named Joaquin, each operating independently in various parts of California, and that their joint crimes were attributed to Joaquin Murrieta.

Greenwood concurred with literary critic Joseph Henry Jackson, who took note of Yellowbird's fantacizing when he wrote an introduction to the 1955 University of Oklahoma Press reprint of *The Life and Adventures of Joaquin Murieta.* While Yellowbird conceded in his thin volume that there were at least *two* Joaquins going under various last names, he claimed that a certain Joaquin Valenzuela was "nothing more than a distinguished subordinate" to Joaquin Murrieta.

Jackson agreed that there "was some foundation for the myth

**Just as there apparently were various Joaquins, there were various spellings of the last name that Yellowbird preferred to spell with one* r *and one* t.

as Ridge put it together." During the winter of 1852 and the spring of 1853, the critic wrote, "it became obvious that far too many Mexicans, perhaps dispossessed miners, had made up their minds to prey upon those who had refused them the right to look for gold." The discriminatory Foreign Miners' Tax Law had been passed by the California Legislature in 1850, making it virtually impossible for anyone but "native or natural-born citizens of the United States" to mine for gold. A "foreigner" had to buy a license (renewable every 30 days) to dig for the stuff. As many of the miners first on the scene were *Californios* or natives of Mexico or Chile who felt they had as much or more right than the newly arrived *yanquis*, their resentment is understandable. Not a few of them turned to cattle rustling, horse thievery and holdups of saloons and lone riders.

"Little was known about these banditti," wrote Jackson, "except the most notable among them seemed all to be named 'Joaquin.' By combining various reports, it was learned that there were at least five such Joaquins, surnamed Carrillo, Valenzuela, Bottilier (or Botilleras), Murieta (sic) and Ocomerena... Whether these men headed separate bands or were members of one, nobody knew. All that was certain was that 'Joaquin' was remarkably ubiquitous. He could drive off fifty head of cattle far down in the great Valley, and at the same hour on the same day relieve a wayfarer of his gold two hundred miles to the north on the outskirts of Angels Camp."

In 1853, a year or two after the teenaged Tiburcio fled into the hills following a fandango brawl, a man identified as Murrieta was killed with several other Mexicans near Tulare by Captain Harry Love, a former Texas Ranger who at the behest of the California governor had formed a posse to hunt down the famed bandit. The posse members rode into Stockton with what they said was Joaquin's head and put it on exhibit, along with a hand that supposedly was that of Anastacia "Three-Fingered Jack" Garcia, presumed by many to be Anastacio Garcia, a friend of

Tiburcio Vasquez. The latter Garcia already had been hanged in Monterey by vigilantes for the killing of a constable during the fandango fight or was yet to be strung up for the murders of two other men--once again, depending upon the authority cited.

So there was a mixup over exactly which Mexican was shot by Harry Love's men in the name of law and order. It is likely that the Garcia done in by the Harry Love posse was only a shirttail relative of the Anastacio Garcia who was Tiburcio Vasquez' friend. Not that many *Americanos* were troubled by the apparent error, or by published reports claiming that instead of killing Murrieta, Captain Love's men had actually killed one Joaquin Valenzuela.

No matter. The Joaquin Murrieta era in California was over--largely because Captain Love *said* it was. The smell of gold had brought armies of *gringos* to scratch at the hills and stream beds. They were not going to let anybody get in their way. It was time for a new Joaquin to lead a revolution against *yanqui* oppressors from the east. Down out of the hills swept Tiburcio Vasquez. He may have seen himself as the savior of his people, but the *Americanos* viewed him as nothing more than a horse thief, cattle rustler and bandit. In any event, he certainly existed, but was not really known statewide until he and his gang raided Snyder's store at the San Benito County settlement of Tres Pinos (subsquently renamed Paicines), where three men were killed--at least two of them by the bandit chief himself. Historian Hubert Howe Bancroft, who seems to have bought the Murrieta legend with few, if any, reservations, wrote of Vasquez:

> Second only in name and achievements to Joaquin Murrieta in the history of California highwaymen stands Tiburcio Vasquez: but except in skill of horsemanship and dexterity in catching and killing men, one was the opposite of the other. Joaquin was of gentle blood, and as handsome and gay and chivalrous as any

> youthful knight-errant; Vasquez was a hybrid, half Indian, coarse, treacherous, brutish. His boyhood was spent in taming wild mustangs, cutting flesh with Bowie knives and shooting, dancing. Indeed, he was a bedeviled Don Juan at Love. Repulsive monster though he was, the dear creatures could not help following him.

"Repulsive monster" was putting it a bit strongly. Vasquez was not really an imposing figure physically, being slightly less than five and a half feet tall. He weighed perhaps 140 pounds without his pistol or rifle. He had a relatively light complexion for a *Californio,* but sported black hair and an impressive mustache. In describing the Vasquez he interviewed in jail following the Los Angeles capture, *Los Angeles Star* editor Ben Truman wrote:

> Take away the expression of his eyes, furtive, sneaky and cunning, and he would pass unnoticed in a crowd. Not more than five feet seven inches in height, and of very spare build, he looks little like a man who could create a reign of terror. His forehead is low and slightly retreating to where it is joined by a thick mass of raven black and very coarse hair, his mustache is by no means luxuriant, his chin whiskers are passably full, but his sunken cheeks are only lightly sprinkled with beard; his lips are thin and bloodless, his teeth white, even and firm; his left eye is slightly sunken...

He was, according to Joseph A. Sullivan in the foreword to Eugene T. Sawyer's biography of Vasquez, a "superb horseman" and a "dandy in dress and appearance." He enjoyed gambling and for a time earned his living as a professional card player around the New Idria quicksilver mines in the hills west of Fresno.

Above all, he was fond of women, which gave rise to numerous stories--many of them no doubt highly exaggerated or invented altogether--of his romantic adventures. He never married. Not that he ever saw the need. There was always somebody else's wife available--even that of his own lieutenant, who eventually avenged that cuckoldry by divulging Vasquez' whereabouts to the law and bringing about his downfall.

Understandably, the capture of Tiburcio Vasquez came as a great relief to the non-*Mexicano* segment of the population. There was intense interest and excitement over the *bandido* who for two decades had eluded posses by melting into the mountains, only to swoop down again with his men upon some isolated town or stagecoach. He usually had his Navy pistol unsheathed or his Henry rifle leveled and had a congenial pleasantry or two for those he was robbing. Despite his low number of known murders, he was regarded by *Americanos* as a cold-blooded killer, especially after the Tres Pinos raid. Yet Vasquez' manners, if the writings of his day are to be believed, were those of a gentleman and he spoke in a cultured fashion. Women were wild about him and a parade of them--including some genteel *yanqui* ladies--visited him after his capture. They packed his murder trial and swooned appropriately at the pronouncement of his doom.

One has to wonder whether Vasquez actually spoke as well as the reporters of more than a century ago would have had us believe. It is possible he did, for he was quite proud of his education. There remain examples of his writing, including a sentimental birthday letter to his son, Rodolfo, and one to his attorney in which he expressed his wish for a change of venue from San Benito County, where feelings against him ran high. All his letters were in his superb penmanship and were couched in flowery language. ("...This statement is not the confession of cowardice but of a conviction that unrestrained public rage has no heart as it has no ears.")

Foreword

Three versions of the notorious *bandido's* life were published within a year of his execution. Ernest R. May suggested in the *Historical Society of Southern California Quarterly* in 1947 that *Los Angeles Star* editor Truman and *San Francisco Chronicle* reporter Eugene T. Sawyer, who covered Vasquez' trial, had written "the most accurate accounts of the bandit's life." As for the book written by George A. Beers, the *Chronicle* correspondent who was with the posse that captured Vasquez, May termed it a "fictionalized account" that could be used as authority "only in regard to Vasquez' capture." Indeed, Beers' book read like a penny dreadful. He packed it with a great deal of obvious nonsense about a supposed childhood sweetheart who continued to love him even after he was on the run. Here is some of it:

> The young robber repaired early to the trysting place and, throwing himself upon the greensward, impatiently awaited the arrival of Anita. As the hour approached, the fair girl appeared--coming with graceful, eager steps--and, entering the thicket of willows, she looked wistfully and anxiously on every side for her lover.
>
> In her dainty mouth she held a pure white rose; her eye was bright with new hope, and her cheeks flushed with pleasure. She had removed her hat, setting free a wealth of dark, curling tresses--as lovely a picture of maiden beauty as the sun had ever shown upon.
>
> As her lover stepped from his place of concealment, her quick ear caught the sound of his stealthy footsteps, and turning towards him, she uttered an exclamation of joy, and bounding forward to where he stood, with arms outstretched and a smile of glad welcome upon his handsome features, she fell upon his bosom and sobbed convulsively for several minutes.

That should be enough of that.

Although there apparently was a young woman named Anita, who took a liking to Vasquez and with whom he attempted to run away--only to get himself shot by her father--there is nothing to suggest that she was the childhood sweetheart reporter Beers decided to award him.

Contradictions, misinterpretations, fictionalizations and just plain lies abound in the various accounts of the life of Tiburcio Vasquez, but it was generally agreed that his outlaw career began on a spring night in 1851 or 1852, when he was 16 or 17 (although he claimed he was only 15) and attended a Mexican fandango in Monterey, Calif. There was a fight. A constable was killed. Vasquez and his friend, Anastacio Garcia, fled. Although some writers insisted that Vasquez was the murderer, he was to claim after his capture years later that he could not recall killing anybody during his entire life. "I am not as bad a man as I am represented," he insisted in his jailhouse interview with Ben Truman. "I have robbed men, and I have tied them up, but I never killed a man, never shed human blood..."

That, of course, put him at odds with just about everyone else on the subject. Official records are sparse. Whether he was a vicious criminal or a gentlemanly revolutionary, this volume represents an attempt to glimpse him in the various lights cast by writers--truthful and otherwise--who have found him of interest during a century and a half.

Perhaps it only matters that Tiburcio Vasquez, the son of respectable citizens in Monterey, was the last major bandit to terrorize California as the new state emerged from the gold rush days.

Vasquez was hanged at San Jose on March 19, 1875. When it came time to die, he did so as a man. "Pronto!" he told the hangman.

Chapter 1

BLOOD AT THE FANDANGO

The first years of my life were spent in the county of my birth in the usual manner of my life and class. My first difficulty occurred in Monterey, in a ball room, when I was 15 years of age. I was engaged in a fight, but no blood was shed.

--Tiburcio Vasquez, in his Los Angeles County Jail interview with Maj. Ben C. Truman, editor of The Los Angeles Star, May 15, 1874.

Although Vasquez was less than truthful in that interview, most writers of the time did not attribute to him the killing of a constable in the fandango hall fight. That night, however, was the end of a peaceful boyhood as he took off for the hills with his friend, Anastacio Garcia, who apparently did the shooting.

Born in Monterey on August 11, 1835, Tiburcio had parents who were honest and hard-working. He was the great grandson of Juan Atanasio Vasquez, who had come from Sonora, Mexico, with the expedition of Spanish explorer Juan Bautista de Anza. Tiburcio's grandfather was José Tiburcio Vasquez, one of the soldiers dispatched from Monterey in 1777 to establish the mission at Santa Clara. José Tiburcio Vasquez married, served as *alcalde* (mayor) of San Jose from 1802 to 1807 and had three sons. One of these, who became major domo of the Mission Dolores, was named Tiburcio and was the uncle of the boy who was to become the terror of California. That uncle received a land grant in what is now the Half Moon Bay area near San Francisco.

The younger Tiburcio's father was Heremenegildo Vasquez, who had been a soldier and had married Guadalupe Cantua of the prominent Cantua land-grant family. For a time, Heremenegildo Vasquez served as a *regidor* (alderman) in San Jose, then moved his family to Monterey, where the Mexican government gave him enough land so that he could make a living growing vegetables.

Tiburcio Vasquez told jailhouse interviewers that he had three brothers and two sisters. Here, again, he was at variance with some historians, although one would think he would be fairly clear on that point. *The Dictionary of Mexican American History*, in which Matt S. Meier and Feliciano Rivera offered some exhaustive geneology, agreed with Vasquez that he was one of six children. Ernest R. May wrote in the Historical Society of Southern California Quarterly in 1947 that Tiburcio's brothers were Francisco, Claudio and Antonio. May said, however, that Tiburcio had only one sister, Antonia, who married a man in Fresno County. May apparently was referring to Maria, whose middle name was Antonia and who married a man named Laria. Dominga Cervantes Hoffer, a one-time Monterey area resident,* credited him with at least two sisters, Maria and Manuela. The latter, Hoffer said, eventually settled down as *Señora* Salgrado on the Anza Ranch. Others said Vasquez had a sister named Dolores.

**Hoffer's study of the life of Tiburcio Vasquez was based on interviews with old-timers in Monterey, some as far back as 1913, but it was not until 1964 that a limited edition was printed in the state of Washington.*

At any rate, Tiburcio appears to have been his mother's favorite. He was reputed to have been almost as devout and as gentle as she during his childhood. He enjoyed music and learned to dance early. Tiburcio attended a school established by General José Castro, where he learned to read and write both English and Spanish well. His penmanship was remarkable and he was quite proud of it. He was something of a poet and could sing, accompanying himself on the guitar. All in all, Tiburcio seems to have led a serene, promising childhood. For a time. Certainly no one who knew him then could have guessed that he would one day become the most sought-after bandit in California.

Under Mexican rule, Monterey had been the capital of California. The governor stayed there when he felt like it. Mexican officials lived inside the adobe presidio wall. But that was before the war with *Los Estados Unidos* and before the discovery of gold had brought the *yanquis* in by the thousands. The town had been a quiet, pleasant place. There were a few dozen adobe and wooden houses scattered outside the wall; a hundred at most. Some were two-storied with balconies from which flirtateous *señoritas* could look down at the *vaqueros* who rode into town for the rodeos and fiestas. The only real violence was an occasional bull-and-bear fight, which particularly amused the pathetic Indians displaced by the crumbling of the missions.

As a small boy, Tiburcio Vasquez apparently had no particular hatred for the *gringos*. The only ones he knew were the traders who had come to make money. Most of them had married the daughters of wealthy rancheros and did not swagger around drunk in the streets insulting people. Monterey's peaceful *Californios* did not suspect at first that these ambitious, energetic *yanqui* businessmen were merely the forerunners of a greedy horde of hellraisers, rapists, thieves and lynchers. There was little about the Monterey of pre-goldrush and pre-annexation days to stir a young boy to hatred. The *yanqui* traders generally got on well enough with the big land grant holders, some of whom had also acquired thousands of acres of secularized mission land that had been promised to the luckless Indians.

The plot of Monterey land that the Mexican government had given to Tiburcio's father was nothing compared to those and it may have been that the boy came to resent that. In any event, Heremenegildo Vasquez had built a pleasant adobe up the slope and enjoyed life with his family.

California life--and thus the life of Tiburcio Vasquez--did not remain peaceful. First there was word of the *Americano* settlers taking over the fort at Sonoma, raising their amateurishly made Bear Flag and declaring California theirs. In Monterey, *Californios* glared as Major John Fremont and other haughty *gringos* galloped through the streets as though they owned the place--which they soon would. Tiburcio Vasquez was not quite 11 years old on July 7, 1846, when United States warships, led by the flagship Savannah, suddenly appeared in Monterey harbor and the *yanquis* came ashore with their rifles to raise their red-striped flag and seize the capital.

As California was ceded to the United States following the Mexican War and as the *Americanos* took over, young Tiburcio began to take an interest in the outdoor activities of men. He was frequently invited to visit the big ranchos of the Castros and his grandparents, the Cantuas. The latter no doubt would have been shocked if they could have foreseen that the well-liked boy would someday be a feared bandit with a hideout in a place called Cantua Canyon.

According to Dominga Hoffer, Tiburcio's principal instructor was Anastacio Garcia, several years his senior and the husband of the boy's foster cousin, Lupe. On the ranch owned by Garcia's family at El Tucho, located where Fort Ord would someday stand, young Vasquez learned to ride, throw a riata, herd cattle and hunt. His parents were said to be happy that he was becoming a man. They were not so joyful, it must be assumed, when they realized that he was spending time with a minor-league *bandido*.

It was about that time that Heremenegildo Vasquez died. Tiburcio, then 13, may have looked to Garcia as a father of sorts. Garcia apparently was a pleasant enough fellow in the beginning, working on various ranchos in the Monterey area and settling down on the bank of the Salinas River with Lupe. But as more and more *gringos* crowded into Monterey, Hoffer indicated, he grew angry and sullen, joining other young *Californios* in cursing them. While Tiburcio enjoyed his company, learning to ride and shoot by his side, Garcia was gaining some reputation as a small-time criminal, holding up lone horsemen in the hills outside of town. After Tiburcio's father died and his mother began to sell tamales and enchiladas out of their small adobe to supplement the income from the vegetable gardens, Garcia would show up frequently to spend some of the money he took from the *gringos*.

The Vasquez adobe soon became a patio restaurant where blue-uniformed *Americano* soldiers and perhaps a few sailors would idle away their time eating Mexican food and drinking *cerveza*. The war between the United States and Mexico was over. The Treaty of Guadalupe Hidalgo had been signed and the *yanquis* were now the proprietors of California. Monterey already had an American *alcalde*, Walter Colton, who had Mexican prisoners from the jail bringing stone from a nearby quarry to erect a fine, big building for the constitutional convention that was to officially organize the State of California. Colton Hall was a mere rock-throwing distance from the adobe where young Tiburcio Vasquez lived, but he did not yet harbor his dream of leading a revolution to drive the *gringos* back across the mountains to the east.

Like almost everything else about Tiburcio Vasquez, there was little agreement about the incident that set him on the road to being a bandit. Despite the concensus of most writers that it was the Monterey fandango brawl, an entirely different story was told by the late Will H. Thrall, an Alhambra man who made a hobby of studying the Southern California haunts of Vasquez. Thrall wrote in the *Historical Society of Southern California Quarterly* of June,

1948, that Vasquez' outlaw career began when he was 15 and living in the town of Sonora in California's gold country. Where Thrall got that information is unclear. No one else spoke of Vasquez living anywhere but Monterey during his boyhood. In Thrall's version, Vasquez "made himself a leader of the younger Mexicans" in Sonora and had "grown bold and arrogant." Said Thrall:

> He had a sister, beautiful and vivacious as young Mexican girls can be, and one night at a dance with him she resented the remarks of an American at the party. Vasquez, claiming that she had been insulted, demanded an apology and in the ensuing brawl stabbed the American.
>
> Fearing the wrath of the Americans and certain retaliation, Vasquez and some of his young Mexican followers fled the town. Soon after this a robbery and murder at a mining camp nearby was laid to him and as he was no longer seen about Sonora it was said that he had joined the band of Joaquin Murrieta, then at the height of his career.
>
> In the mining districts of those days killings were common and, as the victim was perhaps not too well thought of and often the aggressor, they were soon forgotten, so two years later, November 17, 1852, we hear of Vasquez at a dance hall in Monterey where he was the life of the party. When a deputy sheriff tried to put him out, as he asserted for making too much disturbance, a shot was fired and the officer was killed. Vasquez was accused, though it was later determined that another of the party probably fired the shot.

According to Thrall, Vasquez was "now a hunted man with a price on his head," so he gathered together a band of his young cohorts and "launched into a career of holdup and robbery which was to cost many lives and terrorize the southern half of California for more than twenty years."

So although Thrall told of a Sonora incident no other writer seems to have heard of, he at least placed Vasquez at the Monterey fandango hall two years later.

There have been varying accounts of the night at the fandango that launched Tiburcio Vasquez' criminal career. Whatever the precise details, there was a fight--apparently involving Anastacio Garcia and another young man named either Jose Heiguerra, Higuera or Guerra, depending upon whose version one accepts. The popular assumption was that the dispute was over a girl. The statement by Vasquez after his capture nearly 20 years later that trouble was always initiated by boorish *yanquis* trying to push aside the Mexican men and move in on their women suggests there was a *gringo* in the middle of it somehow. At any rate, Monterey Constable William Hardmount (spelled Hardmont by some writers) apparently entered the place and attempted to arrest all three, only to be either shot through the heart or stabbed. There were those who said young Vasquez was the one who killed the officer, but the preponderance of testimony is to the contrary.

In her biography of Vasquez, Dominga Cervantes Hoffer included details that appeared in no other recital. She reported that the incident occurred in 1853 at a hall called the San Juan, "one of many cheap fandango houses in Monterey." She said the trouble erupted when Antonia Romero, "a slender girl with tiny feet and a diabolical, alluring smile," first teased José Higuera, Tiburcio Vasquez and Anastacio Garcia by dancing in front of them as though inviting one or the other to "capture" her by placing his hat on her head in the popular dancehall flirtation exercise. She evaded each of them, Hoffer said, then danced in front of a "golden-haired American seaman" whom she allowed to succeed. Garcia, related Hoffer, had been drinking *aguardiente*, a fiery brandy, and was in a "highly excited state." When the lady accepted the *gringo's* sailor hat, according to Hoffer, simmering *Californio* hatred for *Americanos* boiled over and the fight was on. Most writers said Garcia shot the constable who tried to break it up.

As the officer lay dead or dying on the dance floor, Garcia did not stick around to assist the authorities with their inquiries. Tiburcio Vasquez was right behind him, beginning life as a fugitive. Vasquez was sought for questioning, but was never officially charged. He was to say later that constant hounding by lawmen over the matter was what forced him to stay on the run and to survive by robbing and rustling.

Higuera was not as fast afoot. He was still around Monterey that night when a band of vigilantes got themselves organized to avenge the death of the constable. Hoffer, whose account bore little resemblance to those of other Vasquez biographers, wrote that Garcia and Higuera both were wounded and taken into custody. She said the sheriff, Ned Lyons, allowed Garcia to escape--apparently because he was afraid of him. That so angered the vigilantes, said Hoffer, that they broke into the jail and seized Higuera, hanging him on the spot. Although other writers indicated that Higuera was indeed arrested and lynched by vigilantes, it was generally agreed that Garcia eluded arrest and fled from Monterey with young Vasquez immediately after the killing of Constable Hardmount--only to be captured subsquently in connection with an unrelated double murder and hanged by another group of citizens who also forced their way into the jail.

In a look-back article published several years later, *The Salinas City Index* blamed Vasquez for the killing of the constable:

> About the year 1854, when Tiburcio Vasquez was no more than 15 or 16 years of age, he, in company with Anastacia (sic) Garcia and one Heiguerra (sic), were at a ball given at a Spanish dancehouse in

> Monterey City. Garcia was so drunk, noisy and insolent that complaint was made to Constable William Hardmount, who attempted to arrest Garcia, but was shot dead by Vasquez. Vasquez left at once, but Garcia and Heiguerra remained.
>
> Ned Lyons, who was sheriff, attempted to arrest Garcia, but was deterred by a pistol held by the latter in a threatening manner. While parleying, Jack Robinson came into the room with a shotgun, and Garcia fled--Heiguerra opening the door to facilitate his escape. Robinson put a charge of buckshot into Heiguerra on the instant, and pursued Garcia, and shot him as he ran, one buckshot entering his wrist, causing him to drop his pistol, but he got away.
>
> The next morning an indignant populace took Heiguerra, wounded as he was, and hanged him in the porch of the house where Hardmount was murdered. Subsequently Garcia came and gave himself up, and was examined on a charge of murdering Hardmount, during which it was proven by a number of witnesses that Tiburcio Vasquez fired the fatal shot. Garcia was discharged, but no indictment was ever made out against Vasquez for this murder, although there are witnesses of the affair alive at this day.

Despite the number of details offered by the newspaper, it was not the version most writers accepted--particularly in regard to who shot Hardmount. Nor did others seem to believe that Garcia actually gave himself up. It appears more likely that he and young Vasquez headed for the hills as fast as they could. As for who Jack Robinson was, the *Index* was not a bit helpful.

And, of course, we have Vasquez' own recollection of a slightly more leisurely escape, recounted in Spanish after his eventual capture to reporter George Beers and translated by a Los Angeles sheriff's deputy:

> "About the year 1852, myself and friends were in the habit of giving little balls among ourselves. These balls were frequently interrupted, and the participants rudely insulted and outraged by parties calling themselves native Americans. Whatever their nationality, they were a low order of men.
>
> "From these insults arose my inclination to play the part which I have since acted. The events I allude to transpired in the county of Monterey, and resulted in one or two personal collisions, which, however, passed off without bloodshed.
>
> "At this time I was also charged with having assisted Anastacia (sic) Garcia in a difficulty which took place in a ballroom, in which Garcia killed an employee of the sheriff. This imputation arose from the fact that on the day succeeding the affair, Garcia called on me at my mother's house, and we went off together throughout the country.
>
> "Garcia was afterwards arrested in Los Angeles County and taken to Monterey, where he was lynched by a mob."

In an interview with *The Los Angeles Herald* after his capture at the age of 39, Vasquez offered another version. He said he "went to work" after the fandango hall fracas and that officers arrived to arrest him. "I resisted," he claimed. "A fight ensued and I escaped. No one was killed."

He did not specify what type of job he might have held, although in the same interview he said, "When I lived in Monterey County, I kept a dance house and sold liquor. The Americans used to come in and beat and abuse me and maltreat my women."

(Few of those who wrote about his escapades appeared to take seriously Vasquez' claim that as a teenager he was the proprietor of a fandango hall, although the producers of a 1937 Works Progress Administration history of the Monterey Peninsula apparently accepted it. They said Vasquez opened a dance house and saloon when he was only 15 and soon thereafter, "becoming embroiled with certain Americans who frequented the place, he was obliged to flee the town.")

Asked by the *Herald* reporter what he did after his alleged escape from the officers in Monterey, Vasquez replied, "I took a few cattle and went into the hills near Ukiah, Mendocino County. The officers soon learned where I was and again attempted to arrest me, but after another fight, in which no one was killed, I escaped."

It was only after that, he insisted, that he went to his mother in Monterey and asked her blessing because he was "going out into the world to suffer and take my chances." By that, he made clear, he meant to be an outlaw.

Although Vasquez apparently was to try ranching in Mendocino County a few months later at the behest of his doting mother, the generally accepted version was that immediately after the fandango brawl Vasquez and Garcia rode into the Panoche Mountains in eastern Monterey County, an area that subsequently became San Benito County, where numerous Mexican bandits hid out in remote canyons.

In his fanciful 1875 book about Vasquez, *San Francisco Chronicle* reporter Beers--who was to be in on the capture of Vasquez and to lay claim to wounding him--described young Tiburcio as "an apt pupil" of Garcia, whom he credited with being one of Joaquin's lieutenants. Whereas Joaquin had been motivated largely by a hunger for revenge against the *yanquis*, Beers wrote, Vasquez "evidently took to the 'road' partly in obedience to a born impulse to rob and steal." Throughout his career, Beers said, Vasquez was possessed by "cupidity and an inordinate vanity, which impelled him to desperate adventures for the sake of notoriety, as much as for gain."

Beers may or may not have been correct on that point, but much of his book was plainly nonsense. In describing young Vasquez and Anastacio Garcia (whose first name Beers and several other writers spelled *Anastacia* despite the masculine version offered by historian Hubert Howe Bancroft) Beers created some laughable dialogue:

> "I tell you, Tiburcio," explained the elder of the two, who was riding in advance, "I tell you I'm tired of this dog's life. A vaquero is a slave--a dog! Are we dogs, to slave for these Americanos?"
>
> "Anastacia," was the reply, "I, too, am tired--I want freedom--the freedom of the mountains and the valleys."
>
> "Why, then, idle away more of your youthful years? Why not at once begin the glorious career you have marked out before you? A few bold, shrewd ventures and we may have the means to organize a band that shall strike terror to the hearts of every white household in Southern California. We have a career before us that will make that of Murieta (sic) pale into insignificance."

After being chided by Garcia for his reluctance, according to Beers, Vasquez showed his courage by assisting in the holdup of a passing rider--who supposedly drew a gun and was killed by one shot from Garcia.

However it came about, Vasquez was a figure of violence and lawlessness in California for two decades.

Chapter 2
ON THE RUN

Q. After your escape from the officers in Monterey, where did you go?

A. I took a few cattle and went into the hills near Ukiah, Mendocino County. The officers soon learned where I was, and again attempted to arrest me, but after another fight, in which no one was killed, I escaped.

--Jail interview with editor of
The Los Angeles Herald

Vasquez did not mention anything to his interviewer about the months he apparently first spent in the Panoche range with Anastacio Garcia and Juan Soto, the latter of whom already had a nasty reputation among lawmen.

The early years of Vasquez and his associates have always been blurry for lack of accurate records. At least one historian (Ernest R. May) concluded that Garcia fled to Southern California immediately after the fandango fight while Vasquez remained hidden in the hills for some time. It appears, however, that the two of them went to Saucelito Canyon in the hilly area of what was to become San Benito County, where Juan Soto and other Mexican bandits made their headquarters. There were many small adobes abandoned by luckless miners and these offered shelter to those hiding from the law.

Soto was known to *yanquis* throughout California as "the Human Wildcat," a mean-looking fellow who was a skillful rider and could shoot accurately at full gallop. *El Diablo* himself seemed to peer out of Soto's yellow eyes, which looked in slightly different directions as though he did not want a posse sneaking up on him. With his matted black hair, straggly mustache and angry glare, Soto appeared ready to kill any man he came across for no reason at all. He was said to have murdered several already. As we shall see, he was to be slain in a wild gun battle with Harry N. Morse, the Alameda County sheriff who became famous tracking down California's bandits. Charles Howard Shinn, who apparently knew Morse and who in 1888 wrote a small history called *Graphic Description of Pacific Coast Outlaws; Thrilling Exploits of Their Arch-Enemy, Sheriff Harry N. Morse*, described Soto as

> ...in every respect an extraordinary antagonist. Of mixed Indian and Mexican blood, he stood six feet two, weighed over 200 pounds, and yet was "all muscle," and as agile as a wildcat. His face was most repulsive and full of animal ferocity, inspiring even his own people with dread. His long criminal record of thefts, highway robberies and murders has probably never been surpassed in California.

It was generally assumed that during several months in the Panoche range, Vasquez was Garcia's willing pupil, learning how to waylay stagecoaches or lone riders and live under the open skies. All the while, his anger at the *Americanos* grew. In his jailhouse interview with *Los Angeles Daily Star* editor Ben Truman 20 years later, Vasquez recalled, "A spirit of hatred and revenge took possession of me. I had numerous fights in defense of what I believed to be my rights and those of my countrymen. The officers were continually in pursuit of me. I believed that we were unjustly and wrongfully deprived of the social rights which belonged to us. So perpetually was I involved in these difficulties that I at length determined to leave the thickly settled portion of the country, and did so."

Before going from the Panoche mountains to Mendocino County, Vasquez apparently first went home to Monterey. Perhaps he thought the heat from the fandango incident had cooled down, but he discovered that now--even though not actively wanted for the killing of Constable Hardmount--he was regarded as a hoodlum. It is likely that this was when he encountered the perpetual "difficulties" of which he complained. His mother reportedly set him up with some land in Mendocino County, hoping to turn him into a peaceable rancher. It was then, said Vasquez, that he "gathered together a small band of cattle and went into Mendocino County, back of Ukiah and Fallis Valley." (He did not say whose cattle they were.)

But even in Mendocino County, he was to tell editor Truman, "I was not permitted to remain in peace. The officers of the law sought me out in that remote region and strove to drag me before the courts. I always resisted arrest."

One can only speculate as to the reasons for this alleged constant harassment by law officers, although Vasquez may well have been stocking his ranch with cattle and horses from other spreads. It is not clear how long he lasted as a Mendocino County ranchero, but he told Truman that he finally went to his mother and informed her that "I intended to commence a different life. I asked for and obtained her blessing, and at once commenced the career of a robber."

Ernest May concluded simply that Vasquez was "apparently not adapted to the pastoral life," plainly an understatement. In any event, the bandit recalled for editor Truman that his first exploit "consisted in robbing some peddlers of money and clothes in Monterey County." Next, he said, came the capture of a stagecoach in the same county. "I had confederates with me from the first," he boasted, "and always was recognized as leader."

Vasquez seems to have been active in the horse-thievery business in Monterey County for a couple of years at least. In 1856, some of his men were captured, but he managed to escape. That was the beginning of his reputation for an ability to slip away into the canyons and hills. It may have been around then that Vasquez became known as something of a Robin Hood, supposedly spreading some of the fruits of his horse stealing and cattle rustling among the poor Mexicans of the Salinas Valley. At least that was the account offered by Anne B. Fisher in her history of the area. She wrote that Vasquez hungered for revenge against the *yanquis* and sought by his wits to improve the condition of the poor *paisanos*. This prompted historian May to observe, "Perhaps he sought to improve the condition of only one poor *paisano*, Tiburcio Vasquez." May noted that Vasquez had very expensive tastes--women and cards in particular--and that to finance these recreations he had to steal a lot of cattle. "For this he needed a good-sized band of men," May concluded, "and it is doubtful that he found many men with a talent and an inclination for rustling who possessed as well the Robin Hood proclivities ascribed to Vasquez by the historian of Salinas. In generosity or as a matter of policy some of the stolen cattle were probably distributed for food. The bulk, however, went to one of the markets in the south; and the proceeds went to content the personal passions of Vasquez and his men."

Dominga Hoffer, in her novelized account of the life of Tiburcio Vasquez, wrote that after his first robbery the young fugitive "seemed intoxicated by the occupation of violence." She said, "The ease with which he and Garcia had obtained the money; the excitement preceding the crime; the wild ride to their lair in the Saucelito Valley after the holdup was over; the congratulations and envy of the other highwaymen; the success in hiding their identity, all delighted Vasquez and made him feel thoroughly alive, as a conqueror."

Vasquez so loved gambling that for a time he even tried to make his living as a card player around the New Idria quicksilver mines in Santa Clara County, but did not seem to be particularly good at it and constantly turned back to banditry.

True to his bragging, Vasquez had no trouble recruiting men to ride with him on his forays. He called them his "regiment" and they regarded him as the "captain." At some point, Anastacio Garcia reportedly went south to the Los Angeles area while Vasquez led rustling raids and stagecoach holdups in Santa Clara, Fresno, Tulare and Kern Counties.

As for Garcia, his criminal career was about to come to a violent end at the end of a vigilante rope. After spending some time in the Los Angeles area, he returned to Monterey County, where some said he was active with a group of outlaws called the "Manilas." He supposedly boasted of having killed more than a dozen men. In any event, he certainly was not regarded by *yanqui* lawmen as an upstanding citizen. Although he was still the prime suspect in the murder of Constable Hardmount, Garcia was to be arrested in connection with a matter not at all related to the fandango trouble.

There had been a legal battle going on in Monterey County for several years over the estate of a big land owner named José Maria Sanchez. When he died, $75,000 of his gold came into the possession of William Roach, who had been the sheriff of Monterey County and administered the estate. The details of this episode are not clear, but Roach apparently was not anxious to relinquish the gold, either to Sanchez' widow or to one of his own bondsmen, Louis Belcher, who wanted a share. At one point, according to historian Hubert Howe Bancroft, Roach was jailed, but persuaded the jailer to free him.

Bancroft, in his massive history of California, declared that Anastacio Garcia was one of Belcher's bodyguards. Seemingly at odds with this version was Dominga Hoffer, who wrote that the Roach faction solicited the help of Garcia to settle the matter with Belcher. Perhaps Garcia betrayed his boss. But why the friends of a former sheriff would turn to a bandit like Garcia, who had been in constant trouble with the law and who was believed to have killed Constable Hardmount, is a puzzlement. It is probable that a certain class of *gringos* were content to let sleeping constables lie. It had been, after all, some time since the messy episode at the fandango hall.

At any rate, Garcia and some of Roach's friends encountered Belcher in the barroom of Monterey's Washington Hotel on June 18, 1856. Belcher was shot. As he lay dying, he accused Garcia and the others of the shooting.

Not surprisingly, *yanqui* public pressure began to build to force Sheriff John Keating to arrest Garcia. Either Keating could not find him right away, or he didn't care to for one reason or another. The heat grew more intense, however, with the deaths of two men named Isaac Wall and Thomas Williamson, who were friends of Roach. The circumstances surrounding their murders have never been put in order by the muddled accounts of various writers of the times.

Wall was a former speaker of the state Assembly and Monterey's first state senator. Tom Williamson was a constable whom Monterey history writer Mayo Hayes O'Donnell has described as "popular." Hoffer, on the other hand, referred to the pair of them as "troublesome men...who made a foolish effort to pry from the sheriff the $75,000." O'Donnell wrote that Roach hired Wall as his attorney because *Señora* Sanchez was pressing her efforts to regain the money.

In O'Donnell's version, Wall and Williamson headed south out of Monterey by pack train on Nov. 6, 1856. Whether they had the money and were absconding with it or whether they were going to meet Roach at some location where he had been hiding from Belcher's friends, no one was able to say. It was believed, however, that they did have a large amount of cash with them. On the first night, they made camp at an arroyo about 25 miles south of Monterey. The next morning, their bodies were found in the scattered remains of their camp. Clearly, someone had ransacked their belongings looking for the money.

Anastacio Garcia seems to have gone to a rodeo near Salinas the next day and bragged that he had killed the two men. It took hardly any time at all for the bragging to reach Sheriff Keating, who quickly gathered a posse of deputies and citizen volunteers--perhaps a dozen men. Among them was Charles Layton, keeper of the newly built Point Pinos lighthouse. Another civilian member of the posse was Jim Beckwith, who had only been in Monterey for a few days and was looking for some excitement. Also with Keating was Undersheriff Joaquin de la Torre.

Both George Beers and Dominga Hoffer included in the posse a certain Major Baldwin, whom Beers at one point referred to as "Captain" Baldwin and identified as a Monterey man who simply bore the military title as a nickname.

As told in varying versions, Keating promised the vigilantes in town that he would bring back Garcia dead or alive. The posse rode to the Garcia place at El Tucho, just north of Monterey, arriving there in the foggy darkness of the early morning with the hope of finding him sleeping off a night of drinking. Historical columnist O'Donnell said that when the posse arrived at Garcia's house, the bandit's wife, Lupe, opened the door and claimed her husband was not there. But, O'Donnell wrote, Garcia suddenly jumped out from behind her skirts, shot Undersheriff De la Torre and Charles Layton, then killed Beckwith, grabbed the latter's horse, and fled.

Here is how Hoffer related it in her book:

> Anastacio always expected an attack, and so he had barred the doors and windows with heavy bolts. About a mile and a half from the house, the sheriff's

posse divided into several groups. At first Anastacio did not realize by how many he was surrounded. Major Baldwin and four men made a wide detour and came up in the rear. Charles Clayton, one of Sheriff Keating's assistants, took up a position on the left side of the house. The sheriff and the others were on the right. With Clayton also was Joaquin de la Torre. Both Clayton and De la Torre were eager to have the credit of making the capture. De la Torre had been in several battles in the war of 1846. He liked conflict. He made a rush at the side door of Garcia's house while Clayton attacked the front door.

Apparently Garcia had seen De la Torre or knew his voice, for old Montereyans informed the writer that Anastacio called, "Who is there?"

"Joaquin de la Torre."

"Go away or I'll kill you, thief of Sacramento," warned Garcia.

"Come out and surrender to the sheriff," demanded De la Torre in Spanish.

"I don't want to kill you because you are a Mexican, but if you don't go away, I'll shoot," repeated Anastacio.

"Anastacio, give yourself up," urged De la Torre. "We are a dozen. We'll take you, dead or alive."

Clayton hammered at the front door. De la Torre kicked on the left. Anastacio answered. He opened the front door and fired. His bullet pierced De la Torre's heart. De la Torre fell dead. "Traitor!" shouted Anastacio. "I'll teach you to betray our countrymen to gringos!"

To hear Hoffer tell it, Garcia then wounded Clayton and:

> As the bullets flew, the Garcia children screamed. Their parents commanded silence. Panic seized the posse. When they regained self-control, they advanced forward cautiously and carried off De la Torre and Clayton. Up came the sheriff and his men. They thought Anastacio had several confederates, so rapidly had he fought. In reality, he had only his wife and she was about to become a mother. By his side she stood holding a small, frightened baby, giving him courage.

Hoffer's story was that the posse members tried to drive Garcia out of his adobe house by setting fire to the thatched roof, only to be told by the outlaw that he had placed his children in the attic and that they were being burned alive. Because of a heavy rain the night before, however, the roof failed to burn. Hoffer continued:

> All day the battle raged between the posse and the bandit. Anastacio exhausted his supply of ammunition. He knew that he must try to get away to the willows in the rear of his house. He had to go, and go quickly. He chose to escape through the tunnel, that was dug under ground some years before by him from his adobe house into the willows.

Beers made no mention of any such tunnel, writing only that the posse kept shooting while planning to pile hay up to the eaves of the house and set fire to it. About 5 P.M., said Beers, Sheriff Keating took a bullet in his hat. At the same time, Jim Beckwith, who had been looking for excitement, was severely wounded. (Fatally, according to O'Donnell.) "In the midst of the confusion thus created," Beers wrote, "Garcia sprang from the front doorway and ran at the top of his speed to the nearest timber directly in front of the house."

Whether Garcia had a horse tethered there or whether he grabbed the fallen Beckwith's mount, he managed to ride away in the gathering darkness, leaving his wife, Lupe, and his young children to deal with the posse.

Keating assigned men to watch the Garcia house at El Tucho night and day in case Anastacio reappeared. But he did not. A few weeks later, however, Lupe went into Monterey and made arrangements at the Pacific Coast Shipping Company office to travel south by the new coastal steamer to the port of San Pedro. She told the agent she had decided to leave California forever and take her children--apparently three including the baby--to live with her relatives in Mexico. She paid for the passage in silver dollars and said she would return in four days to go aboard the ship when it anchored in Monterey Bay.

The shipping agent had been in Monterey long enough to recognize her as the cousin of Tiburcio Vasquez and the wife of Anastacio Garcia. Like everyone else, he had heard about the battle at El Tucho and Garcia's escape. He went to Sheriff Keating and told him about Lupe. The sheriff did not believe Lupe was going to Mexico without her husband. It now seemed certain that Garcia was hiding out in Los Angeles County and that she meant to meet him there.

With four days to arrange it and with the *yanquis* so anxious to see the dangerous Anastacio Garcia brought to what they thought of as justice, Keating had no trouble raising money to send someone to Southern California on the ship with Lupe. The only real problem was whom to send. Keating feared that if he sent one of his deputies, Garcia would meet the ship when it docked in San Pedro, recognize the man and disappear forever--even if that meant leaving Lupe and his children stranded.

Sheriff Keating considered various men who frequently joined his posses and finally settled on Tom Clay, an eccentric schoolteacher who had a taste for adventure. Clay volunteered to go. As he looked nothing like a lawman and probably would not arouse Lupe's or Garcia's suspicions, Keating bought him a ticket and sent him aboard the steamer Yerba Buena.

Judging from the writings of Hoffer, O'Donnell and others, schoolteacher Clay turned out to be a fairly good detective, admiring Lupe's children and getting chatty with her by the time the Monterey Peninsula was a low-lying blur astern. Apparently she asked him whether he knew the area around the pueblo of Los Angeles and he assured her that he did, having taught there for a couple of years after arriving in California from Texas. The trusting Lupe told him she had to find the La Brea Rancho. He promised to help her.

When the ship finally anchored at San Pedro, Clay accompanied Lupe and her children ashore on a small passenger boat, then told her to wait for him on the dock while he went to arrange transportation for them. It is probable that as she waited, Lupe sat on her baggage and hoped she would be able to persuade her reckless husband to settle down as an honest *vaquero* so thcy could live a peaceful life. After the green countryside of Monterey, she probably did not care much for the sun-scorched hills she could see rising back of San Pedro. But at least she felt safer here, away from Sheriff Keating and his bloodthirsty posse.

She was to learn quickly, however, that she was being betrayed by her new friend, the schoolteacher. Clay had set off, as ordered by Keating, to contact the local authorities and tell them that Anastacio Garcia was at the La Brea Rancho. A posse found him there and captured him without a fight. He was hauled off to the Los Angeles County Jail and within two days was on the steamship as it made its return voyage to Monterey. His wrists and ankles were in chains and two deputies kept a close watch for every twitch of his face.

Hoffer wrote that Sheriff Keating, who had been friendly with Garcia in the past out of fear of him, met him when the steamer arrived, "took off his handcuffs, shook hands with him and went with him to take a drink." This is a dubious story. It is difficult to believe that the sheriff would be so congenial toward the man who had killed at least one of his posse and wounded two others during the attempt to arrest him at El Tucho. Nevertheless, Hoffer said, this show of friendliness "enraged the vigilantes," who met and decided they would not take a chance on letting Garcia have a trial. How could anyone guarantee what the outcome would be?

In O'Donnell's version, as soon as Garcia was in the Salinas jail he "sent for the men who were responsible for his having murdered Wall and Williamson." We are left to assume that the "responsible" parties were members of former Sheriff Roach's group. Garcia, according to O'Donnell, "threatened to tell all unless he was released." The men, said O'Donnell, "promised to break into the jail that night and free him."

Whatever the exact circumstances, men did break into the jail that night. But they did not free Garcia. Instead, they draped a lariat across a wooden beam in the jail house, put his neck in the noose and tied his feet to an iron ring on the wall. Then they pulled on the lariat until Garcia's neck was broken. The jailer wrote in the Monterey County jail register: "Anastacio Garcia, charged with murder, found strangled in his jail cell this morning, February 17, 1857."

Garcia had hated the *yanquis* so much, and yet had allowed them to make him a part of their plotting. They had killed him like any other Mexican.

Whether the lynching of Garcia had anything to do with it, Tiburcio Vasquez evidently chose that time to shift his operations to Southern California.

That was to lead to his first prison term.

Chapter 3

PRISON AND ESCAPE

In 1857 or '58 I was arrested in Los Angeles for horse stealing, convicted of grand larceny, sent to the penitentiary and was taken to San Quentin and remained there until my term of imprisonment expired in 1863.

Not quite. In talking to editor Truman, Vasquez failed to touch upon the small matter of the prison break of June 25, 1859. But then Vasquez left many holes in his own account of his life.

It may well be that his hatred for the *yanqui* invaders grew sharply with the lynching of his old friend Garcia. It was Anastacio, after all, who had taught him to ride and rope and hunt; who had turned a poetry-writing, guitar-strumming child into a man able to terrorize the *gringos* with the mere sound of his name. Perhaps Tiburcio felt that the vigilantes, having the taste of blood with their killing of Garcia, would now come looking for him. They had almost given up the idea of capturing Vasquez because he had eluded them and the official posses so often. But now that they had caught and killed Garcia after all these years, it was natural that they would think about making a serious effort to hunt down his friend. Vasquez left his Cantua Canyon hideout and rode to Southern California, where it was said he planned to gather a force of men to liberate the state.

When he reached Los Angeles, he found it to be a thriving place; no longer a sleepy pueblo. There was a little plaza and a two-story hotel on Main Street called the Bella Union, where *yanquis* sat under the portico in chairs tipped back against the adobe wall and smoked cigars while telling each other how much money they were going to make. Everything looked quite peaceful, although there had been numerous lynchings of Mexicans and in a few more years there would be a frenzied night in which 21 Chinese would be hanged after the shooting of a white man by a "Chinaman" attempting to protect his own property.

The Pueblo of Los Angeles actually was a rough, lawless place. The Southern Pacific Railroad had not yet arrived to bring businessmen and their families in from the East. There were not too many official lawmen around, but there were vigilantes, who could be far more dangerous because they rarely asked questions before hanging any Mexican they believed guilty of some offense or another. Vasquez probably concluded that he should lie low for a little while before raising his army of liberation. Let the *gringos* forget about Tiburcio Vasquez. They would hear of him again soon enough.

Hoffer wrote that he had "sickened" of the highwayman's life and that for several months he worked on ranches in Los Angeles County. He felt his nerve was gone, she said. She also presented a scene in which Juan Soto, the "Human Wildcat," supposedly came across Vasquez and taunted him for working as "a common *vaquero*."

"I'd rather work like this than be strung up by the vigilantes," the writer quoted Vasquez as telling Soto. She said he also reminded Soto of what had happened to Anastacio Garcia.

To which Soto, she added, responded that Garcia had been a man. "Contempt," Hoffer wrote, "was in Soto's wild animal eyes." That, to believe her version, did it. She related that Vasquez, thus goaded, promptly joined Soto in driving some cattle from a corral on the Santa Clara River and selling them. There is no verification for the assertion that Vasquez' companion was the infamous Soto, although George Beers also said it was he.

Other writers said it was horses, not cattle, the pair stole. Beers wrote:

> On the night of the 15th of July, 1857, Vasquez, in company with Juan Soto, made a descent upon the corral of one Luis Francisco, on the Santa Clara River, Los Angeles County, and stole--as described by the original complaint--*One mule of the value of seventy-five dollars, and nine horses of the value of forty dollars each; and all of the value of four hundred and thirty-five dollars...*

In any event, Vasquez was arrested and indicted. Ernest May wrote that "Tiburcio's *compadre* turned state's evidence and went free." Eugene Sawyer said it was Vasquez who dreamed up a plan to have his cohort "make certain statements" that would free him and that he, in return, "would perform a like service"--only to have his pal testify against him.

Vasquez pleaded guilty and was sentenced to a five-year term in San Quentin Prison, which he entered in late August of 1857. He was only 22 years old.

Inmate abuse was flagrant, because the entire concept was one of making state prisons self-supporting under the control of a private contractor. Until the stone building and a 20-foot-high wall were erected in the 1850s, prisoners had been kept aboard some of the rotting old ships that had brought goldseekers around the Horn to San Francisco. Although some hulks remained in use, San Quentin housed prisoners who worked from daylight to dark making bricks, chopping wood or being farmed out by the contractor as laborers. The abuses became so outrageous that in

1858 the state government cancelled the private management contract and took forcible control. The lieutenant governor became the ex-officio warden.

Apparently Vasquez did not like San Quentin much, later telling a reporter, "I was roughly handled. The treatment was very rigorous." Nevertheless, by most accounts he commanded some respect from the other prisoners, most of whom were *Mexicanos* and who resented the *gringo* laws that put them where they were. To hear Dominga Hoffer tell it, Vasquez constantly was given money by his fellow inmates and he lost most of it gambling. She quoted one anonymous old prisoner as saying, "Vasquez kept them all poor."

According to Hoffer, Vasquez wrote to his mother from prison, asking her to forgive him and to visit. "*Doña* Guadalupe Vasquez never condemned people," Hoffer said. "She had only heartbreaking love for her son... Her one thought was to go to him, take him food and presents." Hoffer said the devoted mother went back to selling Mexican food to raise the funds for gifts and stage fare to San Quentin, finally getting enough. Only to see:

> What a terrible fortress they built for her unhappy boy and other unhappy boys. There would be no chance for any escape from those high thick walls guarded with death-dealing guns. *Doña* Guadalupe did not see the stripes on her son's clothing. She forgot where her boy was. She realized only that after years of blackness and pain, once more they were together. Mother and son sat in the waiting room forgetful of the others, caressing each other like lovers, who love only in the spirit. Vasquez was always at his best when with his mother. Looking at her made him feel like a saint. For these two, words were not necessary. They talked of commonplace subjects because their thoughts were too disturbing for utterance. *Doña* Guadalupe brought

> news of Monterey and of Vasquez' relatives. She asked about his associates, about his food and comforts. She was fearful for him. Tiburcio's answers were rose-colored. His food was the best. His associates were all good fellows. He did not tell her that only iron men could withstand the influence of the prison, that gambling was rampant, that the prisoners cultivated vice and crime, that when a man goes to prison his soul dies...

But as already noted, Vasquez himself apparently was a prison gambler who ruled other inmates by intimidation.

His distaste for confinement became evident on June 25, 1859, when he and 41 other prisoners escaped. Sawyer wrote that the prisoners managed to overpower a prison carpenter, George Lee, and a gatekeeper named John Spell, grabbing Spell's keys. Prison guards opened fire at the fleeing men. Vasquez, according to Sawyer, was shot through the hand.

In Hoffer's account, 11 of the escapees were recaptured, some of them by a sheriff's posse in a ravine at the base of Mount Tamalpais. Two of the prisoners were shot dead as they ran. Several were wounded.

Vasquez managed to get away from the area, traveling on foot--and probably on stolen horses now and then--with a prisoner named Jesús Mendoza. They made it through Solano, Yolo and Sacramento Counties, finally reaching the town of Jackson in Amador County. There, Vasquez stole two horses for them and they were quickly caught nearby. Vasquez was taken back to San Quentin with another year added to his term for stealing the horses.

Hoffer related that Vasquez became involved in another escape attempt only five weeks after his return to prison. She said he was one of about 60 prisoners loading bricks from the San Quentin brickyard aboard the schooner *Bolinas* when they suddenly overpowered a guard on the prison barge. Hoffer said they jumped from the barge to the schooner and tried to set sail. "Unfortunately," she wrote, "they forgot to cut loose the ship from the buoy. The ship was held by a hawser on one side to the buoy and would not move. The breeze swung the ship around and abeam of the prison and broadside to the artillery and the prison." The prison guards opened fire, Hoffer said, and seven prisoners were killed. A dozen more were wounded. The survivors hoisted a white flag.

Verification of that incident was included in a letter that Beers said he obtained from James Towle, acting warden of the prison. Towle told Beers:

> "September 27, 1859, one month and ten days after he returned, he with others seized the schooner Bolinas.
>
> "April 2, 1861, implicated in inciting (another) break, Vasquez stands well among the old prisoners. I cannot find on inquiry among them that he ever showed the 'white feather' here."

For his involvement in the Bolinas break attempt, Hoffer said, Vasquez was "thrown into the dungeon and flogged." For many months, she wrote, he made no further effort to break out. She said the 1861 escape plot was discovered before it could come to anything.

"Finally," said Hoffer, "Vasquez gave up hope of escape before he should finish his term. Revolt died in him. Daily he performed his tasks, also counted the days till the law should give him freedom."

He was finally released on August 13, 1863.

In his jailhouse interview with Ben Truman following his final capture, Vasquez recalled:

> "After my discharge from San Quentin, I returned to the house of my parents and endeavored to lead a peaceful and honest life. I was, however, soon accused of being a confederate of Procopio and one Soto, both noted bandits, the latter of whom was afterward killed by Sheriff Harry Morse of Alameda County. I was again forced to become a fugitive from the law officers, and, driven to desperation, I left home and family and commenced robbing whenever opportunity offered, but always tried to avoid bloodshed."

In another burst of forgetfulness, Vasquez told Truman, "I know of nothing of note until the Tres Pinos affair occurred."

As the violent raid on Snyder's store at Tres Pinos did not occur until 1873, he was passing over a full 10 years of robbery, cattle rustling and horse thievery--as well as yet another stay in San Quentin.

It is true, according to Hoffer, that initially upon release after his first prison term, Vasquez seemed ready to put aside the life of a bandit. She said he was welcomed home by relatives and that the *Californios* in Monterey treated him as some sort of returning hero. Not so with the *yanqui* lawmen, who kept their eyes on him constantly. "In the midst of the joys of the fandangos," Hoffer wrote, "he realized that to the Americans he was the highwayman, an ex-convict, an associate of a man who had been lynched, Anastacio Garcia."

So, said Hoffer, he moved inland to San Juan Bautista, where his mother opened another restaurant serving Mexican food to teamsters hauling loads to and from the New Idria mines.

Sawyer wrote, "His confinement did not produce any change in his morals. He had scarcely got accustomed to the rejuvenating influences of open air freedom before he robbed a fish peddler on the San Joaquin. He was masked at the time, and his victim could give the officers no clue to his identity."

For the next two or three years, with the exception of the apparent theft of some horses in Tuolumne County, Vasquez tried to make his living gambling at the bustling New Almaden and Enriquita quicksilver mines in Santa Clara County. "But Vasquez was either a failure in gambling or else impatient and uncertain of financial return," Robert Greenwood wrote. "In Enriquita one morning, an Italian butcher was found stabbed and some $400 in cash, known to have been in his possession, was missing."

In its 1927 series of articles on the life of Vasquez, *The Hollister Evening Free Lance* said that the victim had been shot through the head as well as stabbed several times in the throat and breast. The Santa Clara County coroner rode up from San Jose to conduct an inquest on the murder. Vasquez was not initially a suspect in the death of the butcher. Apparently, however, he was the only man around Enriquita who was fluent in both English and Spanish. As a result, he was hired as a translator for the inquiry. Whether his interpreting had anything to do with the verdict is unclear, but the inquest jurors listened to testimony and finally concluded that the "deceased came to his death from a pistol bullet fired by some person or persons unknown."

Several days later, according to Greenwood and others, Sheriff John H. Adams "received information" that Vasquez and another man, Faustino Lorenzano, had committed the murder and robbery. But Vasquez had vanished.

From then until 1867 Vasquez was a fairly active bandit, reportedly associating with Juan Soto and Tomas Redundo (or Redondo), alias Procopio--who was also known as "Dick of the Red Hand" and who was a well-known Alameda County criminal. Vasquez was blamed for many cattle and horse thefts in Sonoma, Contra Costa and Mendocino Counties. He was staying some distance from his old haunts around the mines about then. Vasquez was to deny that he rode with either Soto or Procopio, preferring to be regarded as the captain of his own regiment. He did not deny knowing both of them, however.

As always, Vasquez found time for women. One of these was Anita. Several writers agreed upon the existence of this Anita while only *San Francisco Chronicle* reporter George Beers wrote of an earlier one purported to be the bandit's childhood sweetheart.

Unlike the other women with whom Vasquez became involved to his sorrow, Anita was not married. She was the handsome daughter of a wealthy ranchero in the Mount Diablo area of Contra Costa County, a few miles east of San Francisco Bay. It happened in 1865 when Vasquez was riding alone after a presumed visit to a woman. His horse stumbled and fell, throwing him violently to the ground and injuring his arm or shoulder. The ranchero, whose adobe was nearby, took Vasquez in and allowed him to stay there while he recovered. Tending to the injured bandit, who according to writer Sawyer pretended to be an innocent traveler from Mexico named Rafael Moreno, was the lovely Anita.

Vasquez, who had an intense fondness for the other sex, probably found it difficult to believe his good fortune. By all reports, the girl had led a sheltered life and was easily swept away by Vasquez' attentions. Her father, it seems, was not at all pleased and began to regret his own hospitality. As soon as Vasquez was ready to ride, he persuaded Anita to "elope" with him. They sneaked away by horseback in the dead of night, galloping along the road to Livermore. But by morning the angry father overtook them near Mission San Jose. Shots were exchanged between the bandit and the rancher. Sawyer wrote that Vasquez was wounded in the arm and that the rancher recovered his daughter while the bandit rode off to his hiding place. *The Hollister Evening Free Lance* said the girl was struck just above the right temple by one of the shots intended for her lover; that she fell senseless to the ground while the wounded Vasquez fled on his horse. Anita, however, seems to have recovered.

Throughout this period, Tiburcio Vasquez remained active, but generally shifted his operations from one county to another to keep from irritating any one sheriff too much. He was blamed for stealing quite a few head of cattle in Sonoma, Contra Costa and Mendocino Counties. *Yanqui* lawmen generally assumed he was riding with both Soto and Procopio, despite Vasquez' subsequent denials.

In the fall of 1867 he was captured by a posse while trying to run off a herd of cattle in Sonoma County. He was sentenced to his second term in San Quentin Prison. According to Joseph Henry Jackson, the prison records on Vasquez are a little fuzzy because during his first term he was listed on San Quentin rolls as "Basquez." After his escape and his return to the prison in 1859, wrote Jackson, he had been listed as "Tebuzzo Baskes." *Gringo* prison clerks, apparently, were not too comfortable with the Spanish language. Eventually, his record bore the notation: "Same as Tiburcio Basquez who escaped June 25, 1859."

In any event, he apparently did not try to escape during his second term--either because he had decided it was not worth it or because prison officials had improved their security somewhat.

Chapter 4
BACK IN BUSINESS

I made but little money by my exploits. I always managed to avoid arrest. I believe I owe my frequent escapes solely to my courage. I was always ready to fight whenever opportunity offered, but always tried to avoid bloodshed.

Vasquez' second term in San Quentin seems to have been remarkably uneventful, probably because he had no desire to give the *yanqui* guards any provocation to kill him. They must have been aware of his reputation and his standing as a hero in the eyes of the other *Mexicano* prisoners. Nor could the guards have forgotten that he was the apparent ringleader of the mass breakout during his initial stay. Also, Vasquez may have realized that he was by now sufficiently famous that he would be recognized quickly if he did manage to escape again. He was released from his second term June 4, 1870, after three and a half years. He was to tell his eventual captors that it was only then he turned seriously to a life of crime. As quoted by Beers:

> "At the expiration of my time, I returned to Monterey County and resided with my mother, voting in that county. The fact of my having been tried, convicted and sentenced to the state prison caused the people of the county to look upon me with suspicion. This treatment made my position peculiarly disagreeable. To escape from the persecution of enemies, I went to a remote part of the county and went to work on a ranch. Even there my reputation followed me, and the shortcomings of others cast suspicion upon me, to the extent that an attempt was made to arrest me, which I successfully resisted. No blood was shed, and I escaped... From this time I commenced my career as a highwayman."

It would seem, according to Beers' account, that Vasquez was asked to recount his various escapades--and that his reply was somewhat anti-Semitic:

> "It would be almost impossible for me to remember all the robberies I have committed. The first that comes to my recollection is that of a Jew whom I robbed as he was crossing the Soledad River, on his way to San Juan. I left him, his pack and his horse, satisfying myself with his pistol and his purse. The affair passed as follows: I saw the Jew approaching at a considerable distance and stationed myself on the upper side of the wood, concealed in the brush. On the arrival of the Jew, I stepped out into the road, and the moment I confronted him he drew a pistol. I assured him he mistook my intention; that I simply wanted to buy some of his goods, and showed him some money with which to pay for them. Satisfied that I was telling the truth, he unpacked his horse to exhibit his wares, and in an un-

> guarded moment I succeeded in taking advantage of him and disarmed him. Then I obliged him to give up his money. I then mounted my horse and, recommending the adventurous Israelite to ruminate on the mutability of human affairs, galloped away."

Once again, we are asked to believe that Vasquez actually spoke in such terms. It is more likely that Beers was indulging in some of the colorful writing that marked most of his book.

Now that Vasquez was free again, it was widely assumed that he was riding with Juan Soto and Tomaso Redundo (or Redondo, alias Procopio or "Dick of the Red Hand.") As all three were active in the same general area and all were *Mexicanos*, what else were the *yanquis* to think? Hubert Bancroft maintained in his history of California that in the fall of 1870, a few months after his release, Vasquez joined Procopio and Soto; that together they "ravaged the counties of Santa Clara, Monterey, Fresno and Alameda, stages being robbed, ranches plundered, and horses run off in swift and startling succession."

According to literary critic and California history writer Joseph Henry Jackson, Vasquez recruited an outlaw band that included Procopio as well as Francisco Barcenas, whom he had known in prison, and a man named Garcia Rodriguez. It is not known where Vasquez met the latter, but it is quite possible that Rodriguez had also been in San Quentin. Vasquez, as we have seen, denied that his relationship with either Procopio or Juan Soto was anything more than casual friendship. He said he met Procopio in the San Juan Bautista house of Abelardo Salazar, whose wife (as we shall see) was much more than a nodding acquaintance. Vasquez said he encountered Procopio again in San Francisco--which is where Alameda County Sheriff Harry N. Morse was to arrest Procopio and send him to San Quentin, a place Vasquez had no desire to see again.

Regardless of whether Procopio and Soto were in his regiment, Vasquez was so active during the months following his second prison term that Sheriff Morse made several futile excursions into the Panoche range looking for him and the other bandits.

Morse became famous as a hunter and trapper of California outlaws when he finally tracked down Soto and killed him in a gun duel. Soto had been staging numerous holdups, terrifying his victims with his size and wild appearance. Beers wrote that the "sinister expression of his malignant countenance gave some indication of the turbulent passions and the utterly heartless and bloodthirsty character of the man. His eyes were of that nameless hue which can only be approximately described by comparing them to those of a wild animal." Soto had, added Beers, "committed many murders and other outrages, and was considered one of the most dangerous men in the state. He had served two terms at San Quentin."

Soto's final crime occurred on January 10, 1871, when he and two other *Mexicanos* rode into the town of Sunol southeast of Oakland. There, they held up a store owned by Thomas Scott, a former state assemblyman from Alameda County. They shot the clerk, Otto Ludovici, to death. They then ransacked the store and fired a few shots into the rear apartments where Scott's family lived. The Scotts fled to a neighbor's house while Soto and his companions galloped away. Morse showed up and decided from descriptions by the witnesses that Soto was one of the robbers.

It was several months before Morse learned that Soto's hideout was in Saucelito Valley in the Panoche Mountains, about 50 miles southeast of Gilroy. This was a remote area east of Pacheco Pass where a few sheepherders were the only apparent law-abiding inhabitants. There were no roads. Morse made up a posse that included Santa Clara County Deputy Sheriff Theodore C. Winchell, later to serve as Tiburcio Vasquez' hangman. Based on the reports given by Morse and other posse members and recorded by Charles Howard Shinn in his *Graphic Description of Pacific Coast Outlaws*, here is what happened:

When the posse members got to the little valley, they saw three small adobes. Morse thought that Soto's hideout was up the canyon, but he wanted to capture whoever was in the adobes before they could fire off a warning shot. He divided his posse into three groups. Morse walked with Winchell toward one of the houses, leaving his Henry repeating rifle slung on the horn of his saddle because he didn't expect trouble yet.

When he reached the door, he was startled to find Soto, wearing a blue military topcoat and seated at a table with several other men. There were also three or four women in the room. Morse drew his pistol and ordered Soto to put up his hands. Soto glared at him. Morse gave the order twice more. Still Soto did nothing. Morse threw a pair of handcuffs on the table and ordered Winchell to snap them on Soto. The deputy picked up the handcuffs, but the sight of Soto's friends apparently was too much for him. He backed out of the door and left Morse on his own. At that moment, a woman jumped at Morse from behind and grabbed his right arm. A second woman seized his left. Soto sprang up, got behind one of his friends and pulled his pistol. Morse threw off the women and fired once, managing only to shoot off Soto's hat. Soto returned fire and Morse ran out the door. Soto was right after him. They began shooting at each other, with Morse wounding Soto in the arm.

Some writers said Winchell then obtained a double-barrel shotgun and blasted at Soto, who retreated to the house; that Morse ran to his horse and got his rifle. This is not the way, however, that a posse member named Harris saw it. Not in the Harris account set down by writer Shinn, at least. In that version, the event was "a magnificent pistol duel" between Morse and Soto in open ground about the house and corral. As Harris told it, "Soto advanced with a bound, bringing his pistol up over his head, and

Morse, with an almost incredible agility, dropped to ground at exactly the right moment, and so dodged four successive bullets."

Harris went on, "The shots were fired in quick succession, Soto advancing on Morse, every time he fired, with a leap or a bound, with pistol held above his head, and as he landed erect on his feet bringing his weapon to a level with Morse's breast and then firing. After firing he never moved until he recocked his pistol, when, tigerlike, he sprang at Morse again."

When the battle began, Harris said, the two men had been no more than 15 feet apart, with Morse trying to get to his Henry rifle. "I thought Morse was surely hit," recalled Harris, "for his body went almost to the ground; but quick as a flash he sprang erect and returned every shot."

Suddenly, according to Harris, one of Morse's bullets struck Soto's pistol, causing the cylinder to jam. Soto turned and sprang for the adobe while Morse ran toward his horse to get his rifle. All of this occurred within seconds, too quickly for Harris and the other members of the posse to get there. (Where Winchell was at this point is unknown, although he does not appear to have distinguished himself in battle.) Soto secured three other revolvers inside the adobe, then threw off his blue military coat. One of his men put it on to confuse Harris, who was running toward the action. Then, with a pistol in each hand and one in his belt, Soto ran out a back door and sprinted toward his own horse, which stood saddled and bridled beneath a tree. In the excitement, the horse panicked, broke loose and ran away without him. Morse, we are asked to believe, called out, "Throw down your pistols, Juan. There has been enough shooting."

Soto ran for the hillside. Morse raised his rifle and shot him through the shoulder at what Shinn said was a distance of 150 yards. Wounded and further enraged, Soto turned and ran straight at Morse, screaming at him. Harris wrote of the bandit, "I shall never forget how he looked in that terrible encounter. He emerged from the house bareheaded, his long black hair streaming in the wind, and a cocked revolver in each hand."

Morse took aim and fired again, sending a bullet into Soto's brain.

The Human Wildcat was dead.

Vasquez' mother had died by that time. He stayed busy acquiring other people's cattle. Morse was after him as he had been after Soto and as he was still after Procopio. But Vasquez always managed to elude the sheriff by staying on the move and by melting into the canyons and mountains. Too, he was frequently protected by *Mexicanos* who offered him shelter when the posses came around. Miners in the New Idria area and families living on ranches throughout the region of his operations generally pretended that they had never heard of Vasquez when they were asked by searching lawmen.

Free after three and a half years in San Quentin, Vasquez could not help but be aware that his people had grown poorer as the *gringos* got a firmer grip on California. *Gringo* squatters were building cabins everywhere, daring ranchers to try throwing them out. Vigilantes were hanging M*exicanos* who fought back. More and more, the latter were called "greasers" by recent arrivals who felt that *Mexicanos* did not belong in California.

The rancheros, of course, were rulers of the land before the *yanquis* came. They rode across the countryside proudly in their silver-trimmed *pantalones* and deerskin *botas*, or leggings, and with their wide-brimmed hats imported from Mexico--or even vicuña *sombreros* from Peru. For fiestas and other fancy occasions they sat tall in saddles heavy with silver. Many of them had descended from the best families in Spain and they did not want anyone to forget it.

Then someone shouted, "Gold!" and Old California began to die. After the streams ceased to glitter in the sun and the veins had played out, California was left with abandoned diggings, the rotting wreckage of sluicing machines, rusting pick-axes, tumbled-down log cabins and hillsides where only a stubble of stumps remained of the trees. All but a stubborn handful of the miners had given up and had moved down to the growing towns to drink, fight and take their angry disappointment out on the *Mexicanos.*

Tiburcio Vasquez was dreaming of recapturing the land for his people. Among the *Californios* and the Mexicans who had come from Sonora to work in the mines, he was a leader who had stood up to the invaders. He was welcome anywhere in San Juan Bautista because it was about the only town that had not been taken over by the *gringos.* He could ride in on his palomino--which he apparently had stolen from some ranch or another--and could enjoy himself at the gaming tables or with one of the lively *señoritas.* He never had to worry that someone would report his presence to the sheriff. Prominent families invited him into their homes. He stayed most often with Abelardo Salazar, however, because of Salazar's charming wife. She and her friend, Rita Miranda, were--in the words of Dominga Hoffer--the "center of gayety" in San Juan.

How could anyone have expected Tiburcio Vasquez to resist?

Chapter 5
WOUNDED FOR LOVE

Q. Do you think a woman had anything to do with your capture, or in placing officers on your track?

A. (Laughing) No. I never trusted one with information that could harm me.

But they harmed him nonetheless.

Not that he didn't love each of them ardently. As for the wife of Abelardo Salazar, none of the writers seems to have recalled her first name. Perhaps even Vasquez did not, considering the number of women he knew. He probably remembered, however, her copper-colored thighs and the sauciness of her smile. And he no doubt recalled that his affair with her prompted his friend Salazar to shoot him. Even if he had foreseen that, he probably could not have stayed away from her, given his fondness for other men's wives.

In Dominga Hoffer's story, *Señora* Salazar was bewitching and fiery. San Juan Bautista bored her. She was resentful of the church and the way it dampened one's enjoyment of life. Unlike so many other women, she was not at ease going to confession. As Hoffer put it:

> The silence of the town maddened and smothered her. She hated its shadowy, quiet streets. She hated Aves, Hail Marys, the Angelus, the vespers. What a relief to talk to a man like Vasquez! He had not submitted, as had she and other Spanish Californians to being stifled into slavery. He had gone into the highway and protested against conquest. Vasquez had dared life. This weak woman thought that never would she be happy till she, too, had dared. She told Vasquez that she didn't care what happened so long as she lived as Vasquez had lived.

Señora Salazar's closest friend, according to Hoffer, was Rita Miranda, who was related to some of the best California families, but was a "heedless wild woman" who paid no attention to her husband. Rather, she soon developed an affection for Francisco Barcenas, one of Tiburcio's men.

Curiously, this episode in the life of Vasquez did not draw much attention from his biographers, with the exception of Hoffer. Sawyer said simply that Vasquez persuaded Salazar's wife to run away with him, then tired of her and "turned her over to the tender mercies" of Barcenas. In Greenwood's account, Vasquez took her to a town called Natividad, wearied of her in a few days and "abandoned her to her own devices."

Only Hoffer claimed that *Señora* Salazar died as a result of her escapade with the bandit. According to Hoffer, Vasquez went to the lady after staying a few days at the Salazar house and told her he must leave to be about his business. If Hoffer is to be believed, the bored housewife pleaded desperately, "Take me with you, Tiburcio. I am tired of this life. I am dying by inches here. I want to go on the road with you." And when Vasquez pointed out that his life as a highwayman and cattle rustler was dangerous, she is purported to have said, "I love danger. I should adore them with you."

"There are sheriffs," Vasquez supposedly pointed out.

To which she is said to have replied, "I'll spit in their faces. I want to go with you to share all your life."

In this version of the story, Vasquez agreed to take her along while Rita Miranda decided to ride away with them as the companion of Barcenas. While the plans were being made, Vasquez went off for a few days and with two of his henchmen robbed a Monterey fish peddler on his way to San Juan. In the meantime, Barcenas made the final arrangements with *Señora* Salazar. On the night of their departure, she went with him out to the stable on the pretense of showing him a new horse bought by her husband. Rita Miranda was waiting. Barcenas and the two women rode off into the night, meeting Vasquez at a cave in the Pinnacles area east of Soledad near the old road to Monterey. The lovers spent the next couple of weeks in that cave, wrote Hoffer.

For a time, if the story is accurate, both Rita Miranda and *Señora* Salazar had a wonderful time. After the two weeks, the group--including Chievo Arsello, another of Tiburcio's men--moved about the countryside, staying a jump or two ahead of the posses who wanted them for robbery. Friends on ranches in the area kept Vasquez apprised of the law's movements. These included some of the more prominent local residents, such as George Castro, major domo of the Quien Sabe Ranch and a cousin of General José Castro as well as of Rita Miranda. Vasquez was regarded warmly by these *Californios*, who did not see that he was doing anything particularly wrong by preying on the *gringos*.

As the fugitives traveled around the hills that edged the Salinas Valley, *Señora* Salazar's enthusiasm apparently faded fairly rapidly. While Rita Miranda relished life in the saddle, in caves and abandoned adobes, the wife of Abelardo Sanchez soon grew weak and sick, wishing she had never run away from home.

In the meantime, Abelardo Sanchez stormed through the streets of San Juan Bautista vowing revenge. He went into the hills looking for the man who had accepted his hospitality and then betrayed him. He apparently rode through the mountains to Vasquez' old haunts around the quicksilver mines and also asked around Monterey. No one dared tell him a thing. Finally, according to Hoffer, Salazar returned to San Juan Bautista where he found waiting a letter from his wife. She pleaded for his forgiveness and told him she wanted to come back home; that she had made a terrible mistake and would do any penance he demanded if he would only take her back. By Hoffer's account, Salazar wrote to his wife telling her that he would take her back willingly. How such a letter might have been delivered, Hoffer did not say; only that *Señora* Salazar kept it from Vasquez and longed to go home again while her health rapidly deteriorated.

At about this time, Vasquez robbed the Deep Well stage station with Barcenas and the two Arsello brothers, Chievo and Obispo. They were active enough to draw constant attention from sheriffs and posses in the area. Vasquez was considering shifting his operations south, to Lake Elizabeth near Los Angeles. One of his brothers, Francisco, was a justice of the peace in that area. Vasquez probably assumed that would afford him some protection from the law. To quote Hoffer:

> "I am not going," said *Señora* Salazar.
>
> Vasquez stared at her. It was the first time that he heard rebellion in her voice. She showed plainly that she meant what she said, but she trembled with dread of what was to come.
>
> "Why?" Rita exclaimed. "What has got into you?"
>
> "She's joking," said Vasquez.
>
> "No, I am going back to San Juan." Her eyes glittered, and she coughed.
>
> "You are not going back to San Juan," said Vasquez.
>
> *Señora* Salazar was calmer. "I am."

The Hoffer account included a lot of other improbable dialogue involving a supposed near-duel when Barcenas, whom Hoffer called *Bassinez*, urged Vasquez to let the woman go. Then, Hoffer wrote, the end came for the poor lady:

> *Señora* Salazar threw her arms around Vasquez' neck in a weak condition which gradually crept upon her during this excitement, but he would not listen to her protests. He could not credit the truth. He flung her aside, and again he moved toward Bassinez with a pistol. Then *Señora* Salazar fell to the ground. Vasquez thought she fainted. He tried to bring her back to consciousness, but the feeble, passionate and feverish life had departed so quickly. Vasquez and his company were alone at night with the dead.

Hoffer said Vasquez and his friends then sat around trying to decide what to do with the body. Barcenas and the Arsello brothers, Hoffer wrote, rode to the nearby ranch of a friend named Cayetano Lugo and explained the predicament. A Lugo relative, Francisco Blanco, was dispatched to the bandit encampment with a spring wagon and tools to construct a rough coffin. He was to carry the corpse of *Señora* Salazar to her husband in San Juan Bautista. Blanco promised to take care of everything and suggested that Vasquez and the others vanish, but Vasquez didn't, preferring to "do the decent thing by their friend," the wasted *señora*. In fact, said Hoffer, Vasquez, Rita Miranda, Barcenas and the Arsello brothers all followed the wagon to the Lugo ranch and knelt in prayer for her there while the body was laid out and dressed in black. Francisco Blanco then carried the remains of the late departed lady to San Juan, where he parked the wagon in front of Abelardo Salazar's home.

> He rapped at the entrance. Abelardo came to the door. He was just eating supper. Blanco did not know what to say. He pointed to his spring wagon. "Your wife..."
>
> Abelardo's face lighted with joy.
>
> "Yes, she's coming back. I brought her." Blanco pointed at the wagon.
>
> At last Salazar understood that something had happened. Stupefied, his eyes were fixed on the rough hand-hewn box. Blanco in a low voice said, "Vasquez sent her."
>
> "Vasquez killed her!" shouted Salazar.
>
> "No, she was weak. Her heart gave out," explained Blanco. "She died on the plains of Salinas from fright when Vasquez and Bassinez were having a fight."

Whether that unlikely conversation actually took place as she relayed it, Hoffer claimed that a San Juan Bautista old-timer told of remembering that *Señora* Salazar was taken to the San Juan Mission for mass and burial. "At last she had her wish," Hoffer wrote. "She had come back to her love and to San Juan Bautista."

It was the death of *Señora* Salazar, Hoffer said, that triggered a sudden spurt of indignation against Tiburcio Vasquez, who had been a popular man with the *Californios* of San Juan and environs. Until that unhappy episode, Hoffer said:

> The easy-going people of that community had shown tolerance for his misdeeds. All were his well-wishers. They knew his family. They were attracted by his pleasing manners. He killed no one. His crime was the harmless one of robbing Americanos, they said to each other. After the death of *Señora* Salazar, who was one of their own people, even the Spanish-Californians

believed that they had overdone their kindliness for him.

Vasquez apparently encountered Abelardo Salazar one evening outside a San Juan Bautista blacksmith shop while talking with a couple of friends. Salazar, probably because he knew Vasquez was in the vicinity, was armed. Hoffer wrote that Salazar accosted Vasquez as follows:

> "I want to speak to you. I am no murderer. I'll give you a chance for your life. You stole my wife. You killed her. Get into the street and defend yourself."
>
> Vasquez laughed. He did not move. Salazar fired. Salazar's first bullet struck Vasquez' vest and he felt a sting upon his stomach, but he was protected by the coat of mail. Vasquez' shot missed. Vasquez' friends claim that Vasquez did not try to hit Salazar, but it is more probable that his aim lacked its usual certainty of marksmanship because of the excitement of the moment. For several seconds in the main street of the town the duel went on. Salazar shot without hatred. He shot to kill. He struck Vasquez on the right side of the neck and the bullet came out below the shoulder. Blood spurted forth. Immediately Vasquez' companions carried him away, as they thought he was dying.

One must question Hoffer's claim that Vasquez was wearing a "coat of mail" fashioned for him by a man who had learned the art in Spain. She attributed that information to a certain Juan Chavarria, who was 87 when she interviewed him in 1913.

As in most other aspects of Vasquez' life, the various writers differed sharply over what happened to the outlaw after he was wounded by Salazar. Greenwood noted that Salazar swore out a complaint against Vasquez and that a grand jury quickly issued an indictment, "but Vasquez had vanished into the Panoche mountains."

Others wrote that Vasquez, who was to bear the bullet scar on his neck for the rest of his life, was carried into the blacksmith shop and spirited out of San Juan Bautista in a wagon before he could be arrested for the wounding of Salazar. Hoffer wrote that the "weak and wounded" Vasquez was taken to the home of his sister, Manuela, who by that time was married to a man named Salgado, on the Anzar Ranch.

As soon as he was able to ride, according to Hoffer, Vasquez left the ranch in the dark of night and made his way to San Francisco to catch a steamer to Mexico. It is possible that this account had some basis in a Mexican sojourn that others say came sometime later, in the spring of 1871, after Vasquez was seriously wounded once again--this time during a gun battle with a posse. No other writer offered the San Francisco story told by Hoffer, who said that while waiting to board the steamer, Vasquez hid in the home of Guadalupe Larios de Salas, who lived in an upstairs flat on Kearny Street. *Señora* Salas, Hoffer noted, was the daughter of Manuel Larios of San Juan Bautista, a remote cousin of Vasquez--as numerous residents of California seemed to be.

As is long since obvious, it is impossible to know what was true or false in much of what was written about Vasquez. When it came time to go to the ship taking him to Mexico, Hoffer said, Vasquez disguised himself as a woman and took a streetcar to the dock in order to evade detection by the police.

At any rate, the *Señora* Salazar affair was over. As had happened when he had attempted to run off with the lovely Anita, Vasquez had been wounded because of his involvement with a woman.

Once again he had survived, but he was not always to be so lucky. The time was coming when an affair with yet another man's wife would lead to his doom.

Chapter 6
GUN BATTLES WITH THE LAW

I know of nothing worthy of note until the Tres Pinos affair occurred.

In his eventual jailhouse interview with Ben Truman, Vasquez seems to have been somewhat forgetful. Perhaps he simply saw no need to tell the reporter all he knew about himself before his trial. At some point during that period, for example, came his apparent sojourn to Mexico. It is uncertain whether he went there soon after being shot by the jealous Abelardo Salazar, as Dominga Hoffer claimed, or after being wounded by a marshal during a subsequent attempt to capture him. Most writers of the day preferred the latter account.

If that version is correct, he remained for a time after the Salazar affair in Cantua Canyon, gathering some of his old compatriots around him while he recuperated. These included Francisco Barcenas, who apparently had decided to put aside his resentment at the captain for having taken Rita Miranda away from him. It is not known what became of *Señora* Miranda, although Dominga Hoffer said she remained with the Vasquez gang for a year or so, then wearied of the life and remarried.

Vasquez went back into action, robbing the Visalia stage at Soap Lake, 12 miles north of Hollister. With him were Barcenas and one Narcisso Rodriguez. The driver and his passengers were relieved of their money, then were tied up and left lying face up on the ground to stare at the bright sun, treatment that became Vasquez' trademark and prompted a great many complaints. In Hoffer's account, however, Vasquez displayed during this holdup one of his more chivalrous moments when a woman passenger began weeping as she relinquished her watch and a $20 gold piece. Vasquez told her to keep them. He even untied her hands. She then pleaded, "Please don't hurt my husband."

"Which one is your husband?" Vasquez supposedly asked her, then ordered the lucky gentleman to "sit down by your wife." His hands were also untied. The other passengers were not so pleasantly treated. They remained tied and were relieved of more than $400.

Later on the same day, Vasquez was riding alone near San Juan when he encountered Thomas McMahon, of Hollister, driving a horse-drawn buggy. McMahon operated a Hollister general merchandise store and was the son of the proprietor of McMahon House, a pioneer hotel. Apparently it had reached Vasquez that McMahon had been in conversation with Alameda County Sheriff Harry Morse, who wanted his help in capturing Vasquez. McMahon knew Vasquez by sight and had promised Morse he would report to him anytime the bandit showed up in the area. Vasquez, one gathers, decided to teach McMahon a lesson. The following, according to reporter George Beers, is the way Vasquez himself told of the encounter when interviewed by Beers in jail years later:

> " 'How are you, Tom?' said I.
>
> " 'Very well, friend Tiburcio,' he replied.
>
> "I then inquired if I had ever done him any harm. He replied that I had not. I then told him that I had learned of his underhanded dealings with Morse, and

> that I proposed to repay him in his own way. Upon being called to deliver, he handed over his coin and a fine improved Colt's revolver. I then informed him that I wanted a fine ring that ornamented his handsome hand. To this he rather objected, but on being informed that I would stand no nonsense, he made a virtue of necessity, and he and the ring parted company. Then I told him I was no assassin; I would make him a present of his cowardly life, which he was by no means loathe to accept, with permission to jog on with his fine buggy and horses."

It is difficult to believe that the bandit actually addressed his victims in this manner. Robert Greenwood wrote that Vasquez got $750 in cash from McMahon, who apparently had another $500 in a shot sack hidden beneath the seat of the buggy. When Vasquez read about that in the Hollister newspaper, he is said to have vowed to take the $500 out of McMahon's pale *gringo* hide if he ever ran into him again. McMahon, on the other hand, supposedly never traveled alone again without a double-barrel shotgun.

Reporter Eugene Sawyer wrote of later asking Vasquez about the reported threat against McMahon, only to be told, "No, I never tried to get even on McMahon, though I had plenty of chances to do so if I had felt inclined. I know that he gave Abelardo Salazar $300 to try and catch me. Salazar, instead of acting like a man, ran off to Mexico with the money."

Asked by Sawyer how he found this out, Vasquez supposedly replied airily, "Oh, I have friends all over the southern country, and I have always been posted in regard to every move planned or directed against myself."

On the same day of the Soap Lake stage robbery and the holdup of McMahon, Vasquez and his men also robbed the stage between Gilroy and San Juan Bautista, only to encounter some gunfire from resentful citizens as they rode toward Gilroy afterward. Beers quoted Vasquez as telling him that the shooting by unhappy residents actually prompted him and his men to abort their plan to hold up the Gilroy stage and "to strike for the mountains, successfully eluding our pursuers and making good our escape." *The Hollister Evening Free Lance*, however, indicated that the three bandits also found time that day to hold up three or four teamsters on the road to Hollister.

Here, according to Beers, is how Vasquez described what happened next:

> "We then directed our course along the mountain range to those hills lying immediately around Monterey. I spent several days on a ranch, resting, amusing myself with dancing, etc., with the *señoritas*. Here, I was attacked by Sheriff Tom Wasson (of Monterey County) and a party of fifteen men, who captured eight of my horses and outfit, including my arms. I escaped, of course, on foot. I struck into the mountains and lay perdu for more than a month, during which I succeeded in renewing my mount with the best of horses, saddles, etc."

The rash of holdups had *Americanos* in that part of the state upset, primarily because Vasquez had tied up the stage passengers and had left them lying on the ground with their faces to the sun. Sheriff Wasson probably had organized his own posse because he felt that Alameda County Sheriff Morse was not doing a very good job of finding Vasquez. At least Morse hadn't caught him yet and the voters were no doubt disturbed.

Wasson's posse came upon Vasquez' camp in the hills while the leader was sitting around the fire with Barcenas and Rodriguez. The bandits heard the snapping of twigs and branches as the lawmen tried to sneak up on them. The trio dove away from the firelight into the shadows and immediately there was a gun battle in the trees. Vasquez and Barcenas managed to get away in the darkness while the posse members fired wildly after them.

Rodriguez was not so fortunate. He was captured on the spot and soon thereafter sentenced to 10 years in San Quentin for his part in the robbery of the Visalia stage. He deprived the *yanquis* of their full satisfaction, however, dying only two years later of an overdose of prison alcohol.

Vasquez and Barcenas were joined in the hills by Gracia Rodriguez, who was Narcisso's older brother. Informed by them that Narcisso had been captured, Gracia swore that he would break into the jail and free him. Vasquez had to calm Gracia down by pointing out the obvious difficulties in such a scheme.

A few weeks after he was almost captured by the Wasson posse, Vasquez was in the Watsonville-Santa Cruz area with Barcenas when there was another run-in with the law--this time resulting in a serious wound. Although some accounts indicated that this confrontation involved a second posse, Vasquez seems to have remembered it as a shoot-out with a single officer. Beers wrote that Vasquez told him:

> "I remained at Santa Cruz some days unrecognized, when my presence became known to L.T. Roberts, the marshal. One night early, as I was riding through town with one of my companions, a resident of the place, Roberts emerged from a house to halt us. I was on the opposite side of my comrade, when Roberts sang out, 'Stop!'
>
> "Reining my horse back and wheeling toward him, I sang out, 'Never!' Simultaneously we exchanged shots. His bullet struck me under the right armpit, passing out back near the spine. Mine struck him in one of the legs. My companion and myself succeeded in gaining a secure hiding place in the mountains where my wound--at first exceedingly

painful--soon healed, and I was once more ready for business."

Writers of the time said Vasquez rode 60 miles that night, even though wounded. *The Free Lance* said he was "Nearly dead from loss of blood" and was "about the gamest man ever seen." The bullet had entered just below the nipple and had come out under his right shoulder. He was bleeding heavily. But he kept going until he reached Cantua Canyon, where he found some of his old friends. They tended to him and he settled down to heal.

Within a few days of this, according to *The Free Lance*, Barcenas was shot and killed by officers in Santa Cruz County.

Vasquez, meanwhile, spent several weeks recuperating in Cantua Canyon, not far from the New Idria mines, knowing that Morse and the other sheriffs were searching hard for him from Monterey to the Panoche Mountains. There was scarcely a day that he did not hear of inquiries being made around San Juan or the quicksilver mines. It was only a matter of time, he must have known, before somebody would tell the *gringos* where to find him.

It probably was at this point that Vasquez--once again recuperating from a bullet wound--went to Mexico. Some writers said he made the trip with Procopio. That does not seem to be entirely accurate. Although Procopio apparently was there at the same time, they do not seem to have gone together. It is logical that both men chose to go south of the border for a time. The wave of holdups as well as the killing of Juan Soto by Morse in the famous gun battle had heightened the interest of various lawmen in Vasquez and other bandits. The heat was on.

It may well be that Vasquez went to San Francisco and from there to Mexico by ship as Hoffer wrote--although she seemingly tied the trip to the wrong shooting. There does not seem to any substantiation for Hoffer's claim that Vasquez hid in the San Francisco home of Guadalupe Larios de Salas while waiting for the steamer and that he went aboard disguised as a woman. Vasquez, by most other accounts, was much too *macho* for that.

Beers wrote:

> Shortly after the killing of Soto by Morse... Vasquez and Procopio, thinking the country was getting too hot for their safety, concluded to emigrate to Mexico. The proceeds of a couple of robberies and $500 given Vasquez by one of his brothers, a respectable citizen of Monterey (at one time a justice of the peace), gave them the necessary funds--the $500 from the brother on the bandit's solemn promise never to return to California. Vasquez professed regret that he had brought sorrow on his relatives, who were living respectable lives, and vowed that he would never return to the state.

The brother referred to by Beers is believed to have been Francisco, who by then was actually living in the Elizabeth Lake area just west of the present city of Palmdale in Los Angeles County. Another brother, Antonio, who also pleaded with the bandit to remain in Mcxico, was living in Carmel, Monterey County.

While in Mexico, it is said, Vasquez went by the name Ricardo Cantua, using his mother's family name. Despite his vow as cited by Beers, Vasquez does not seem to have concerned himself too much with the wishes of his family and whether his banditry might embarrass them. He undoubtedly found life in Mexico boring, with no rich *gringo* bankers or rancheros to waylay and no adulation from *paisanos* seeing him as a revolutionary hero. In California, he was Tiburcio Vasquez the general, the commander of a regiment. His people needed him. He was a *Californio*.

Then, there was the small matter of conscription in Mexico. Hoffer wrote that he was offered an officer's commission in the

Mexican army, but that he declined the honor and went back to California, preferring to be a highwayman. Beers' version was that Vasquez was conscripted into a Mexican regiment "and was obliged to appeal to the American consul at Guaymas to effect his release; that the consul then told him that he had best leave the country at once and return to California, as he was liable to be conscripted at any time, and perhaps it would be impossible to again effect his release." That, at least, said Beers, was the excuse Vasquez gave to his brother for having violated his promise to stay south of the border.

Comes at this point another episode of which only Dominga Hoffer seems to have known anything: the supposed fathering of a child by a young Southern California woman. In Hoffer's words:

> Few knew of the existence of the child. Those few who know do not tell the name of the mother. She was an innocent girl of a respected California family in the Elizabeth Lake country. Her father was a wealthy ranchero. She was one of the many *señoritas* and *señoras* that gave Vasquez reason to boast, "I never married, but I always had the woman I chose."

The young woman, whom Hoffer fittingly elected to call "Modesta" for purposes of her story,

> ...was young, nearly 20 years younger than Vasquez, very innocent and devout. Seldom did she leave her father's ranch. She met only Spanish Californians and she heard nothing but good of Tiburcio Vasquez.

As Hoffer told it, there were rumors that Vasquez was once more in California and a posse was out looking for him. He took refuge in the Elizabeth Lake region, where the friendly ranchero told him to remain as long as he wished. Because rewards were being offered for information leading to his arrest, Vasquez stayed away from the ranch house, apparently sleeping in the open nearby. The ranchero's family, said Hoffer, sent him food. Foolishly, they allowed Modesta to carry it. Hoffer related:

> To the young girl Tiburcio Vasquez was a dear friend secreted in the forest, homeless like the wild animals, wronged, man-hunted, persecuted. Modesta pitied Vasquez. She prepared him delicious Spanish dishes. Three times a day she filled her basket with food and carried it to him. The poor man was so grateful that she was touched to tears. Once he kissed her hand. No man had ever kissed Modesta's hand...
>
> Then he slept and she watched. While he slept she noticed that the lines on his face deepened. She was filled with pity for him. So soundly did he sleep that she thought he would never know if just once she gave him a kiss on the cheek as if he were a puppy, a kitten or a doll. She was so young and so much of a mother that she still had a tenderness for dolls.
>
> Her kiss woke him. He held her in his arms and she could not stop blushing. Women known by Vasquez were not given to blushes. Modesta's blushes maddened him. She tried to run away. She explained that she was playing he was her white-nosed puppy, but he did not hear her explanation. Drunk with his kisses and his sweet, intoxicating lies of love, she left him. Each day she went back and listened to more lies. Vasquez returned to his raids in the north and left her sobbing her grief, but hoping for his return.

Within the ensuing year, Hoffer wrote, the ranchero who had sheltered the bandit "was surprised to learn that Vasquez had violated his hospitality." Modesta, it seems, gave birth to a baby boy. Hoffer wrote that when Vasquez heard of this event, he was very happy and "made a wild ride south" to see his son, "talked the matter out with the indignant ranchero" and promised to send the infant to his own relatives. He apparently never did, for Hoffer quoted an unidentified cousin of Vasquez as saying that on the day he was hanged in 1875, the bandit told her, "If you ever see my son, be good to him."

Vasquez gave credence to the story when he told *Los Angeles Daily Star* editor Ben Truman after his capture, "I was never married, but I have one child in this county a year old." He left behind a letter to *my idolized son on his birthday.* In this exquisitely penned message, apparently written from jail while awaiting his trial for murder, Vasquez called the boy Rodolfo and spoke in flowery terms of his love and pride. *(I kiss your baby forehead...)*

As usual, however, stories, dates and known facts do not jibe. Vasquez' apparent stay in Mexico and his supposed dalliance with "Modesta" would have occurred in 1871. He was not captured and interviewed by Truman until three years later. So perhaps he fathered some other child. Vasquez seemingly did not feel inclined to clear up the matter.

Chapter 7
ADIÓS, PROCOPIO

Q--In what part of the state have you committed your robberies, or most of them?

A--In Santa Clara, Monterey, Fresno and Los Angeles Counties. I have committed many robberies in those counties, but do not wish to name them or give details.

Sitting in his cell in the Los Angeles County Jail after his eventual capture at Greek George's place, Tiburcio Vasquez obviously enjoyed talking to the various newspaper reporters who begged for interviews. But with a murder trial awaiting him in San Jose, he saw no reason to furnish his prosecutors with more information than they already had or leads to crimes they may have linked to some other *Mexicano* bandit. At any rate, his criminal career (or revolutionary crusade, as he saw it) had become more intense after his return to California from Mexico.

In Eugene T. Sawyer's version of Vasquez' comings and goings, the bandit arrived in San Francisco by steamer, which may or may not rule out the supposed time he spent in Southern California impregnating "Modesta." It is possible that he simply took the ship from San Pedro to Northern California after that alleged dalliance.

In either case, his old pal Procopio also had come back from south of the border and was hanging around San Francisco by the time Vasquez showed up. It is likely that the two of them did a little carousing, but Vasquez always denied that he and Procopio committed robberies together.

Procopio was reputed to be a cousin of Joaquin Murrieta. His criminal career reportedly began in 1862 with the murder of Los Angeles area rancher John Rains. The latter was shot and lassoed from his horse near what became the Los Angeles suburb of Azusa. His body was dragged into the bushes, where it was found the following day. There were rumors that Procopio and others had been hired by a Californian named José Ramon Carrillo to kill Rains. It was never known why. Carrillo denied any connection and was released for lack of evidence. Another suspected accomplice, Manuel Cerradel, was arrested, convicted and sentenced to 10 years in prison. While he was being taken to San Quentin, however, vigilantes hanged him from the yard arm of a steamer.

Procopio moved to the Livermore Valley in Northern California, where he began to associate with several other well-known bandits. Robert Greenwood wrote:

> Procopio was tall, slender and handsome, with brown hair and brown grey eyes, a cool, cunning, slippery customer, but no evidence could be obtained. He went into the Santa Clara Valley on many cattle stealing expeditions, and after one of these was arrested at Alvarado, but shot the officer in the arm, swam the creek and reached the willow thickets. He was closely followed by a number of armed citizens, and a running fight ensued. When his ammunition gave out, he surrendered, and got a long term in state prison.

No sooner was he released, than Procopio went back to stealing cattle and horses as well as to robbing stage coaches in Monterey, Tulare and other counties.

The relentless Alameda County sheriff, Harry N. Morse, was still on the trail of both Procopio and Vasquez. One night, hearing that Procopio was drinking and dancing at a certain *Mexicano* saloon in San Francisco, Morse marched in. He simply walked up to Procopio, put a gun to his head, grabbed him by the throat and said, "You're my man. Let's go." When Procopio seemed ready to draw his pistol, Morse reportedly told him, "I don't mind killing you, Dick. It'll save the state a lot of money. Go ahead and try."

Procopio was probably not as daring as he had been earlier. His first stay at San Quentin and years of running from posses no doubt had taken something out of him. He decided not to draw. Morse walked him out of the place at gunpoint. Procopio was convicted of grand larceny for some adventure or another and was sentenced to 14 more years in prison. He never rode across the hills of California again.

Tiburcio Vasquez was now the only famous bandit left in the state.

Vasquez repaired to his old haunts in Cantua Canyon and picked up where he had left off, holding up stages and lone riders as well as an occasional store. He came and went as he desired around the New Idria area mines, always protected by the miners and even the mine officials, who saw no reason to incur his wrath. One time, it was said, three lawmen went to New Idria to capture him after hearing that he could be seen riding around openly or playing poker. The officers visited the mine superintendent, who with a straight face told them he did not know where Vasquez was, that he had not seen him recently. The lawmen searched for several hours, questioning Mexican and Chilean miners and offering to pay a reward for information leading to Vasquez' arrest. All pretended either not to know where he was or *who* he was.

When the three gave up and decided to ride back to San Juan Bautista, they had to go up a hillside. On the far side of the creek was a small adobe. A man was watching them from the window. They saw him and kept riding, having no idea that he was the one they sought--Tiburcio Vasquez.

The lawmen camped that night near the Panoche Valley. When they awoke in the morning, their horses were gone. It was generally assumed that Vasquez and his men had taken them. Indeed, Sawyer quoted Vasquez as saying later, “Smart boys. I saw them all the time they were looking for me, and when they left, I made up my mind to play a trick on them, and I am sure they knew where their horses went to.”

Several attempts to capture Vasquez at the mines were made by Sheriff John Adams of Santa Clara County during this period, but the miners always protected him. Once or twice deputies reportedly went there disguised as peddlers or as men seeking work--only to have Vasquez learn of their approach, probably from friends or relatives close enough to the sheriff's office to find out what was afoot.

By most accounts, Vasquez moved freely back and forth from his hideout to the dance houses and saloons of Hollister and Gilroy, where he enjoyed the poker tables and the company of women. He always managed to leave before word filtered out to the *gringo* lawmen that he was in town. In one case, he carelessly remained the entire night in Hollister and was engaged in a game of casino with one of the women when what Eugene Sawyer called “a law-and-order Mexican” reported his presence to an officer. A posse was hastily formed, but Vasquez saw them coming and was able to sneak out the back way, riding away casually.

One of Vasquez’ nieces, Concepción Espinosa, was living in Benito, south of Hollister, with José Castro, who kept a saloon. Vasquez apparently felt relatively safe there. Hoffer wrote that Castro occasionally rode into Hollister on Vasquez’ behalf to ascertain whether there would be any valuables in the express box on the next stage. "If things looked favorable," she said, "Castro spurred his horse the 25 miles so as to arrive before the stage in order to give Vasquez the word that the time was ripe for a holdup. Whenever Castro was seen riding toward San Benito, the stage drivers knew danger was ahead."

But, Hoffer said the old-timers in the area claimed, Castro was reluctant to participate in the actual holdups, until "persuaded by force." Sawyer wrote that Vasquez "taunted him with cowardice" and that Castro then drew a pistol. "The light of Tiburcio Vasquez would have been then and there extinguished," Sawyer related, "had not the cap of the pistol snapped without igniting the powder." According to Sawyer, there ensued a hand-to-hand struggle that ended with Castro vanquished. "A reconciliation took place," said Sawyer, "and the saloon keeper finally agreed to lend his assistance to the nefarious project. One other man, whose name Vasquez did not disclose, was induced to join."

The San Benito stage was held up several miles from Castro's saloon. A large sum of money was reported taken. Later, several riders were held up along the road. When the news reached Hollister, there was, in Sawyer's words, "great excitement and a company of vigilantes was quickly organized." Vasquez, as was his habit, vanished from the scene. It did not take the vigilantes long, however, to find José Castro, try him on the spot and lynch him.

Vasquez made a raid soon thereafter in Peach Tree Valley, where he ran off some cattle belonging to the wealthy Henry Miller. After that, he spent four or five months in what Sawyer called "masterly inactivity," lying low in Cantua Canyon and other hideouts while the posses searched for him.

By January of 1873, Vasquez had begun organizing what he probably thought of as the cadre of a regiment that would eventually free his people from *gringo* oppression. His base was in Cantua Canyon at the home of his first recruit, Abdon Leiva, a Chilean who had been working at the New Idria mines.

It was there that Vasquez met Leiva's wife, Rosario.*

With their first exchange of glances, Vasquez' doom was sealed.

**As virtually all of Vasquez' biographers of the time spelled Señora Leiva's name* Rosario *rather than* Rosaria, *that spelling is used here.*

Chapter 8
"A CRIMINAL INTIMACY"

Q--Tell me about the affair with Leiva's wife.

A--A criminal intimacy had existed between myself and Leiva's wife long before I left the ranch in Monterey County, but Leiva never suspected us.

Perhaps Vasquez would not have considered recruiting a Chilean for his regiment if it had not been for the wicked eyes of the man's wife. He probably never would have seen those eyes if he had not run into Abdon Leiva in 1873 while lying low in the Mexican camp at the New Idria mine, where Leiva worked as a blacksmith. Vasquez was invited to visit the little ranch at Chilaro where Leiva lived with his wife and children.

Vasquez may have heard about Rosario Leiva. She was said to be one of the better dancers in Santa Clara County. Since Vasquez regarded himself as a fine dancer, he no doubt looked forward to meeting her. He may also have heard that Leiva mistreated her. If so, that probably disturbed him, for there is no record of the bandit ever hitting a woman. Indeed, he undoubtedly appreciated high spirits and took pride in being able to command a female's respect without physical abuse. Although Rosario eventually was to charge him with endangering her life and abandoning her in the mountains, Vasquez would have pointed out that she chose to go with him and had only herself to blame.

When he first met Rosario at the Leiva home, the two apparently hit it off instantly. Rosario, like the wife of Abelardo Sanchez before her, appears to have been bored with her life and titilated by the presence of the famous highwayman and cattle rustler. According to Hoffer, Vasquez arrived just as Leiva was visiting some sort of abuse upon Rosario and demanded that he stop. Leiva supposedly apologized.

As Hoffer told it, Rosario Leiva was no raving beauty, but was slightly on the plump side with a faintly pockmarked face. Nevertheless, she apparently had bright, tantalyzing eyes and a charming smile. She had enough, it seems, to prompt Vasquez to remain many hours that first evening at the Leiva house, chatting and dancing. Rosario, based on the accounts of old-timers interviewed by Dominga Hoffer, was the granddaughter of Ignacio Alviso, who had come to California with the De Anza expedition in 1776--as had Vasquez' own grandfather. The bandit apparently seized upon this to convince her that their meeting was preordained.

She had married when she was 17 and had spent most of her married life on the small ranch not far from the New Idria mine. Vasquez was from Monterey--a desirable quality in itself as far as the mountain country *señoritas* were concerned--and was better educated than her husband. In addition, he was a genuinely charming man with social graces beyond those of Leiva, the Chilean blacksmith. Although Rosario was the mother of two children, she was still young enough to enjoy going to fandangos. She and Vasquez danced at many of them together. Just what her husband was doing all that time is not clear.

More from Hoffer on the subject:

At the mine fandangos he never left her side. In every act, word and tone he told her that he was her adorer. Echoes came to Rosario of women who had loved Vasquez and had been deserted by him, but he told her that he had never loved the others. With her he desired to be forever, but his life and liberty were always in peril. Never when he closed his eyes did he ever know whether the next morning he would be behind bars, or whether he should be hanging by the neck on a greased rope from a tree.

Nothing he had to offer her but his love. That he gave her on his knees one evening after she had danced the *jaravo* at the New Idria mine fandango and made all the miners cheer. As he helped her on her horse he kissed the tip of her small scarlet satin slipper. Rosario had tiny feet and Vasquez had the slippers sent to her from San Francisco. The flame-colored, embroidered crepe shawl draping over her shoulders was also a gift from him.

The next morning Rosario Leiva left her children with a neighbor and rode with Vasquez to the top of a distant mountain peak. It was a wonderful ride through a coppice of manzanita and buckeye upward over the barren mountain with its red brown sides that told of the approach to the great New Idria quicksilver mine. Sure-footed horses took Vasquez and Rosario easily to the very summit of the mountain. Suddenly they came upon a golden field of mustard, yellow foget-me-nots and orange poppies.

It was spring and the pair sat down there and talked all the radiant day until the sun set in a jonquil horizon. Vasquez told Rosario of his life, how he lived each day as it it were the last. She tenderly warned him of the dangers always at his heels. He didn't mind

> death, he answered. Death was everywhere. Dead insects were there in the poppies. Perhaps they had died because they were too happy. Not far away was a dead jackrabbit. What could be more beautiful than to sleep in the mustard, forget-me-nots and poppies as the jackrabbit was doing? Vasquez didn't mind turning into a blade of grass or a poppy or a tree. All he asked of life was to have one supremely happy day with Rosario.

From then on, it appears, the smitten Rosario worked on her husband to help Vasquez in his fight against the *gringos*. She complained that she was fed up with being poor and with seeing Leiva come home each night tired from his forge at the mining camp. When her husband protested that Vasquez was a bandit and cattle rustler, she pointed out that if the *gringos* had not come to take away her mother's land, she would be rich. How was it robbing, she wanted to know, to take back from the *yanquis* what they had stolen in the first place? And no doubt she threw up to Abdon the fact that he was a Chilean, which explained why he did not feel strongly about what had happened in California.

At last, Abdon Leiva agreed to ride with Vasquez--on one holdup, at least. He probably was more interested in winning back his wife's affection than in living a life of danger. Perhaps if he became a daring bandit, she would stop talking about Vasquez. He must have suspected already that what Vasquez called "a criminal intimacy" existed between them.

As previously noted, Vasquez was gathering the nucleus of the band that would be with him through his major exploits. A Frenchman named August de Bert, who already had ridden with him a few times, appeared at Leiva's ranch and re-enlisted. Teodoro Moreno, who had been shearing sheep for a distant cousin of Vasquez on a ranch near Gilroy, also decided he was tired of working hard and wanted to share the excitement.

Another recruit was young Cleovaro Chavez, whom Vasquez had known in San Juan Bautista. Chavez' aunt was married to another of Vasquez' relatives. He was only 23, but he was tall and strong and he had admired Vasquez since he was a boy. He was anxious to become part of the revolution. He had a light complexion, gray eyes and thick, black hair. He wore a goatee and short whiskers on the sides of his lower jaw. He had thin, bloodless lips and a scar on his cheek. He was a daring, tough man who was to become Vasquez' lieutenant.

There was another early member of what Vasquez called his regiment--a hunchbacked Frenchman who had been working at the New Idria mine and who was called "Horbada." He soon disappeared. His bones were found in a cave in Cantua Canyon, which was the site of Vasquez' headquarters. There was a rumor that Vasquez had ordered Horbada killed because he got drunk and talked too much in the saloon at New Idria. If that was the case, it was never proved.

Vasquez appears to have intended, once his spring-of-1873 campaign was over, to move to Southern California where he would publicly declare his revolution against the *gringos*. Then, "*El Capitan*" was probably sure, the regiment would become an army and what had been a few bothersome robberies would be the forerunner of a full-fledged war for the freedom of California.

The first big raid to be made by the newly formed regiment of Tiburcio Vasquez was at the settlement of Firebaugh's Ferry on the San Joaquin River in Fresno County. Vasquez had heard that Henry Miller, the prominent San Joaquin Valley cattle baron whose ranch already had been visited by the bandit, was going to Firebaugh's Ferry to deposit $30,000 in cash at the general store to pay his men. Miller was known to ride around with a sack of gold. Once before, according to Hoffer, Vasquez had encountered Miller on the road and had relieved him of some of it. Miller supposedly showed no resentment at all, but had simply borrowed $20 from

Vasquez and had gone on his way. Hoffer said the cattleman eventually repaid the $20 when he ran into Vasquez in Gilroy.

Firebaugh's Ferry seemed to Vasquez a good place to begin the revolution in earnest. With him were Leiva, Chavez, De Bert and Moreno. Leiva and Moreno had not taken part in robberies before and were understandably nervous. By this time Vasquez had acquired a beautiful palomino horse that was to be his trademark throughout California. The ranchero who lost it must have been angry, but it was important to Vasquez that he have a stately mount on which to lead the cadre of what he believed would become a mighty army. He undoubtedly knew he cut a fine figure as he and his men rode into Firebaugh's Ferry late in the afternoon. He intended to be quite a lot richer by nightfall.

There was nothing much there other than the store, a livery stable and a few houses. There was not even a decent saloon where a man could refresh himself. Unfortunately, he quickly learned from the storekeeper that Miller had not shown up as expected, so the $30,000 was not on hand. The storekeeper was very disappointed, because he had anticipated doing a lot of business with newly paid *vaqueros*. His disappointment was nothing compared to that of Vasquez, who decided upon the spot that it should not be a wasted trip. He and his men held up the store.

There were perhaps a dozen men who had come in from ranches around the valley to buy provisions. Three or four of them were *vaqueros* who probably had been waiting for Miller to show up so they could get their pay. Vasquez and his men drew their pistols and ordered all of them to lie on the floor. The victims were hogtied with rope from the storeroom so they could cause no trouble. Their pockets were searched, but the robbers found only a few hundred dollars and a couple of gold rings. Vasquez ordered the storekeeper to give him the combination to the safe or be shot between the eyes. The man was quick to oblige. But all Vasquez found in the safe was another $500 or so.

While the robbers were still searching the store for anything of value, the stage arrived. The driver and his passengers also were robbed at gunpoint and tied up on the floor of the store with the others. The stage's box yielded a small amount of gold--a few hundred dollars worth--and some meaningless papers headed for a bank in Fresno. The passengers were not carrying much money or jewelry, so the gang gained little more.

By Hoffer's account, Vasquez also pushed his way into the storekeeper's adjacent house, startling the man's wife, who was in bed. Perhaps she was not young and attractive enough for him, because there is no record that he joined her in bed. This is how Hoffer told it:

> She screamed when she saw him. "Where is my husband?"
>
> "In the store."
>
> The woman started to go toward the door.
>
> "Don't go," said Vasquez. "You are undressed."
>
> She had less concern for her appearance than he. "I don't care. I am going to my husband."
>
> When the merchant's wife saw her husband bound hand and foot, she flung herself upon him and wept bitterly. She turned to Vasquez. "You are not bad enough to take the watch my husband gave me when he was courting me."
>
> This kind of appeal never failed to reach Vasquez. "No," he said. "I am not so very bad." Then he handed her the love token. One of his company protested against his liberality in returning a $300 watch, but Vasquez commanded silence.
>
> The merchant was so grateful for the watch that he asked his wife to fetch for Vasquez his own watch and said, "You have not such a bad heart after all."

Another version of the watch story was supposedly told by Vasquez himself and passed along by author Robert Greenwood, who said the story was "worth nothing, the type of story often told of outlaws intended to picture them as romantic and generous." The fact that the story was reputed to have been told by Vasquez himself, wrote Greenwood, "gives us some insight into his conceit."

Here, as quoted by Greenwood, is the purported Vasquez version:

> "I took a watch away from a man named the Captain. His wife saw me and, coming up, threw her arms around my neck and begged me to return the watch; that her husband had given it to her during their courtship and she couldn't bear to part with it. I gave it to her and then she said, 'Come with me.' I followed her into another room, and from behind the chimney she took out another watch and gave it to me. The Captain said, 'You haven't got a bad heart after all'."

As Greenwood said, "We can only speculate whether Vasquez is really the proper source of the story. In such matters it is best to let the reader judge for himself."

Vasquez and his men rode away. They had not got the $30,000 they had been expecting, but they had a little something for their trouble. And their reputation was growing quickly. They returned to the Leiva house in Cantua Canyon, where Rosario no doubt enjoyed knowing that her husband was now part of the gang. Leiva, however, was not happy about it, fearing capture at any moment. He probably knew that most *Mexicanos* in the area were aware his house was the hideout. It apparently did not make him feel any more secure when one of the banditti, De Bert, suddenly rode south in the direction of Mexico, perhaps also sensing that it was only a matter of time before they all were caught.

Hoffer related yet another story that no other writer seems to have known anything about. She wrote that Leiva drank too much wine one night at the mine and shot an innocent bystander to death during a quarrel. Leiva, said Hoffer, fled to his ranch, but there were threats to lynch him--not only for the killing, but because he was rumored to have been part of the Firebaugh's Ferry robbery. Vasquez, according to the Hoffer account, went with Leiva back to the mine, where Vasquez confronted Leiva's accusers. Hoffer wrote:

> When these men saw that Leiva was a friend of Vasquez, they came forward, shook hands with Vasquez and said that what Leiva had done was of no consequence. "We don't want to disturb you boys," said Arthur.
>
> "And we won't bother people here at the mine," promised Vasquez. "I give you my word." There was general handshaking...

Greenwood noted that various writers spoke of the apparent agreement between Vasquez and the mine superintendent under which the latter would not give lawmen any information about the bandit's movements as long as Vasquez did not rob the mine or its employees. On one occasion, Greenwood reported, Vasquez and Cleovaro Chavez, who by now had become the bandit leader's second in command, stopped the New Idria stage and ordered all the passengers out, only to discover that the superintendent was among them. Vasquez ordered everyone back into the coach and sent them on their way without robbing them.

It was not only the superintendent who protected Vasquez. As *The Hollister Evening Free Lance* noted:

> The officers were informed on many occasions that Vasquez could be found at or near the New Idria mine, and several attempts were made to capture him, but without avail. The Mexicans who constituted almost the entire population of the mine and the mountains adjacent were, with but few exceptions, partial to Vasquez.

Hoffer said that during the evening following the showdown with Leiva's accusers, Vasquez attended a fandango and fiesta at the mine with both Leiva and Rosario. It was the first night since the Firebaugh's Ferry robbery, Hoffer wrote, that Abdon Leiva was able to sleep. The next morning the three of them went back to the Leiva house, where Vasquez began planning a new and daring robbery--that of a Southern Pacific Railroad pay car.

It was to be one of his less successful ventures.

Chapter 9
THE NOT-SO-GREAT TRAIN ROBBERY

When I wanted a party of men I had no difficulty in finding the requisite number. The work done, the party disbanded and each went his own way. I trusted no one.

That was generally true during the early part of Vasquez' career. But by the time of the Firebaugh's Ferry raid, he had a cadre on which he intended to build an army of liberation. Young Cleovaro Chavez became a fixture as his lieutenant.

It was the summer of 1873 that the two of them began planning to waylay the Southern Pacific train between Gilroy and San Jose so they could rob its pay car. Vasquez knew that the train came from San Francisco at the end of each month with money to pay the railroad's employees along the line. He no doubt was excited at the thought that such a holdup would make him famous east of the Sierra as well as in California. Perhaps he even thought the United States government would conclude that its new state was too dangerous for *yanqui* settlers and would return the golden land to its people.

The plan was simply to loosen one of the tracks near an inn called Twenty-One-Mile House, derailing the train. Then Vasquez and his men could clean out the pay car and gallop off into the hills. It seemed an exciting prospect for the seizure of a sizeable amount of cash. Leiva appears not to have gone along on this expedition, probably still nervous about following a life of crime. Vasquez settled for a small company that included Chavez, a former prison associate named Blas Bicuna and Teodoro Moreno, his sheep-shearing cousin from Gilroy. There were six others.

The band rode to a place known as the Divide, where they selected a good hiding place to tether their horses. Then they set about to remove one of the tracks with crowbars. The writers--as usual--differed on what occurred that day. Greenwood said that either the bandits had not given sufficient time to removing the rails to derail the train, or the railroad had been told about the robbery plan and had re-scheduled the train.

Hoffer wrote that Vasquez later learned from a man living in San Juan Bautista that "the railway officials had discovered their plan and were on guard."

The Hollister Evening Free Lance, in its 1927 feature on Vasquez' career, offered a downright racist account:

> The characteristic laziness of the Californians delayed their preparations and, as the train was ten minutes ahead of time, the affair was an utter failure. As the train approached, the members of the chosen band were busily engaged in damaging the track. It came thundering down and passed them as they sprang back, and whisked out of their reach ere any harm could be accomplished.

Whatever caused his failure to stop the train, Vasquez was determined not to return to the hills empty-handed. He decided to rob the patrons at Twenty-One-Mile House, much as he had expressed his disappointment by holding up the Firebaugh's Ferry store when Henry Miller did not arrive with his $30,000. Vasquez probably wanted the *gringos* to understand that it was not wise to keep him from the money and gold he felt belonged to the people of California.

For her version of what happened, Dominga Hoffer relied on the 1913 recollection of a certain John Horne, who worked on a ranch belonging to the hotel. To hear Horne tell it, Vasquez and his men rode abreast down the Watsonville Road, all masked with black mufflers. About a mile from the inn, they came across a *yanqui* teamster. As they did not want to have anyone riding off to report to the sheriff their presence in the immediate area, they tied him up and threw him over a fence, where he lay undiscovered until morning.

Vasquez and his men then rode on to the inn, where they dismounted. Sitting on the porch were four men, identified in the Horne-Hoffer account as Horne himself, barkeep Newton Finley, Archie Tennant (brother-in-law of the proprietor) and a sewing machine salesman named Perkins. The Chinese cook was in his cabin at the rear of the hotel. "Go into the barroom and lie down," Vasquez commanded the startled *gringos*. Perkins, thinking it was a joke, started to laugh. But when Vasquez pulled a revolver and pointed it at him, he stopped laughing and went with the others, getting down on the floor without a word.

Vasquez left Chavez standing guard at the doorway so that no one could come upon them by surprise. Then Vasquez and the rest of his gang tied the victims face-down with rope found in the storeroom behind the bar, going through their pockets and the cash drawer. There were only a few dollars in the latter, so Vasquez put the muzzle of his pistol close to bartender Finley's head. Finley insisted there was no other money in the place, but changed his mind when the hammer of the revolver was pulled back with a chilling click. Vasquez then had Moreno untie the feet of Finley, who led them to a trunk hidden behind some whiskey cases in the storeroom. In it was about $60. "That's all there is," he said.

Counting what they took from pockets and cash drawer, the bandits got only about $200 along with some watches and rings. It was a dismal profit compared to what Vasquez had expected from the SP payroll car.

After he stopped Moreno and one of his other men from drinking too much free whiskey at the bar, Vasquez led the band away. The Chinese cook emerged from his quarters and untied the victims. Horne and Finley then rode to the next inn, Twenty-Mile House, to tell about the robbery.

The following account appeared in *The Gilroy Advocate* of August 2, 1873:

> Last Wednesday night, about 8 o'clock, Mr. Finley, who has charge of the Twenty-One-Mile House during the owner's absence in Europe, two farmhands and a traveling agent for a sewing machine, who were stopping there for the night, were seated in the barroom of the above wayside inn, when six Mexicans rode up, watered their horses, dismounted and entered as though for a drink. Such was not their purpose, however, for after a little maneuvering they drew their pistols, covered the unsuspecting inmates with them, and with the admonition to be quiet and make no resistance, they proceeded to bind them. The two farmhands and the machine agent were laid on the floor, bound and covered with a blanket. Finley was bound, and the leader of the gang holding a knife in most uncomfortable proximity to him, demanded to know where the money was, remarking that unless the information was forthcoming he would be dispatched to Davey Jones' locker. A second demand was not necessary, and the desired information was imparted instantly. About $155 in

> money was taken, together with four watches. One was taken from Finley, a fine silver watch, which he had purchased from H.C. Warner, of this city, a short time ago, and one from the sewing machine agent, together with what loose change he had upon him. Luckily, the other two men had nothing valuable on them. After securing this booty one of the ruffians helped himself to something to drink, and the whole party mounted their horses and rode off in the direction of this city.

The *Advocate* said that next to the holdup at Firebaugh's Ferry, this was "the boldest robbery which has occurred in this vicinity for a long time." It called for immediate measures "to hunt out this band of lawless marauders and bring them to speedy justice."

Despite the fact that the Santa Clara County sheriff was now searching for Vasquez and his men in earnest, Hoffer wrote that they happily dropped in on a dance at Warm Springs, near Gilroy. Nor was that the end of Vasquez' celebrating, according to Hoffer, who said that "with all the countryside looking for the robbers, Vasquez rode into San Jose on horseback, attended a fandango and was the hero of the festivities."

Within a few days, Hoffer wrote, Vasquez, accompanied by Bicuna, "rode back to Rosario on the Cantua Creek to prepare for the fatal raid on Tres Pinos, which cost Vasquez his life later."

By Hoffer's account, the bandit leader was so disgusted and frustrated by his failure to rob the Southern Pacific pay train that he was determined to carry out three other robberies in rapid succession. These were to involve Snyder's store at Tres Pinos, the New Idria stage and a store on the San Benito River. Vasquez talked about his plans with Chavez and with Rosario, according to Hoffer, "but when the subject came up, Leiva walked out of the room." He apparently was determined not to participate in any more crimes, because people had been eyeing him suspiciously ever since the Firebaugh's Ferry raid. Rosario supposedly continued to urge her husband to help Vasquez, fearing that the latter might go away and leave her.

Also, according to Hoffer, Rosario had become pregnant by Vasquez, greeting him with that joyous news when he returned from San Jose. If that indeed was the case, it was not made clear how Vasquez felt about it. He did, however, persist in his efforts to keep her husband riding with his band. Leiva was still reluctant, pointing out that he would not be able to continue living in the area; that he would have to sell his small ranch and few cows so he could move himself and his family out of California.

"Leiva," Tiburcio Vasquez was quoted by Hoffer as saying, "if you don't lose your nerve, you'll have something to leave the country on. I know there's a lot of money in Snyder's store and on the New Idria stage. It will fix us all comfortable for life. You needn't worry about a mortgage after that. Sell out cheap before we start. Then you can buy land on the other side of the Colorado River. I know where you can find plenty of land."

Leiva purportedly said he still would not go along, but when he walked out to tend to his cows, Rosario told Vasquez, "He will go. His 'no' means 'yes'."

Chapter 10
VIOLENCE AT TRES PINOS

I told them not to use any violence, as when I arrived I would be the judge, and if anybody had to be shot, I would do the shooting. When I arrived there with Chavez, however, I found three dead men, and was told that two of them were killed by Leiva...

The robbery of Snyder's store at Tres Pinos on August 26, 1873, had more to do with making Tiburcio Vasquez notorious than any of his other crimes. Until that bloody episode, he was simply one more Mexican outlaw plaguing the *yanqui* settlers. But at Tres Pinos three innocent men were killed, something that had not happened before in his career. Suddenly, he was known throughout California as a violent, bloodthirsty criminal rather than as a genial Robin Hood exchanging pleasantries with his victims.

Although he was to claim--as in the above jailhouse statement to newspaper editor Ben Truman--that he killed no one, witnesses swore otherwise. He apparently shot at least two of those who died at Tres Pinos. He was to be convicted in one of the deaths. As he was still facing trial when he talked to Truman,

Vasquez attempted to blame two of the killings on Leiva, who had turned state's evidence against him. No doubt Vasquez was astonished that Leiva could betray him. After all, hadn't Vasquez shown great affection for Leiva's wife? Did the man think so little of the honor?

As already noted, Vasquez anticipated taking quite a lot of money from the store at Tres Pinos. He meant to then move his operations to Southern California, where he could launch his campaign to defeat the *Americano* invaders. While planning the Tres Pinos raid and hiding out at Abdon Leiva's little ranch in the La Cantua area following the abortive pay train job and the holdup of Twenty-One-Mile House, Vasquez continued to pressure Leiva to sell his property and to move Rosario and the two Leiva children to Los Angeles County. They were to be stashed at the Lake Elizabeth area ranch of a man named Jim Heffner, who appears to have been on friendly terms with various outlaws. Vasquez, it might be assumed, wanted to be certain that Rosario would be waiting for him in Southern California. Leiva, having got into some sort of trouble with the mine bosses at New Idria, at last did as he was urged.

Rosario and the children were sent south in a wagon said to have been driven by the son of Joaquin Castro, on whose ranch Vasquez and his men had stayed occasionally when posses got too close to Cantua Canyon.

Tres Pinos* was at the junction of the San Benito and New Idria Roads. There was a hotel and Andrew Snyder's store, which had a barroom. As it was a stage station and chief watering place for horses, there was a windmill and pump which kept a trough running full. Almost everyone going to and from the Panoche and New Idria quicksilver mines stopped at Tres Pinos. Vasquez understood that there was always a good deal of money

**Tres Pinos subsequently became the town of Paicines, with the name Tres Pinos transfered to another settlement nearby.*

on hand at Snyder's. He had been there many times and was well known around the place. Perhaps he wanted to be recognized when he held it up. It probably annoyed him that *The Gilroy Advocate* had not even mentioned his name in its account of the robbery at Twenty-One-Mile House.

Hoffer pointed out that no one around Snyder's had ever thought of trying to arrest Vasquez because it "was considered quite a thing in that vicinity to leave Tiburcio alone so long as he left the natives alone. If the sheriffs of Santa Clara, Monterey and Santa Cruz wished to have the recreation of chasing Tiburcio Vasquez and his men, that was no man's affair but their own."

After seeing Rosario and her children off for Southern California, Vasquez and Abdon Leiva met Romulo Gonzalez and Teodoro Moreno at the house where Vasquez' sister, Maria, lived with her husband, Manuel Laria. They did not stay long, apparently because Maria was perceptive enough to know that something was afoot and she was nervous. The bandits then camped in a small canyon about a mile from Tres Pinos, cleaning their weapons and getting ready. Vasquez had his Henry rifle and Navy pistol as well as a big knife. Chavez had a double-barreled shotgun. He also carried two revolvers.

In his attempt to lay much of the blame for the Snyder's store killings on Leiva, Vasquez told reporter George Beers:

> "I made it a special condition that Abdon Leiva should take command for the occasion, because it became necessary that he should go into the place in the daytime, reconnoiter, and make the necessary dispositions, and that I would make my appearance at night. At five o'clock of the evening of the 26th, I sent Leiva and Romulo Gonzalez ahead, with orders that they should enter the town, take a few drinks and smoke a few cigars, and ascertain the inmates of Snyder's store, and they were not to do anything until my arrival...

They started, and in a short time I sent Moreno, and about dark I followed with Chavez."

Leiva and Gonzalez walked into the store as planned. The New Idria stage had just arrived and store clerk John Utzerath was sorting the mail it had brought. Leiva and Gonzalez ordered drinks and cigars, as instructed, and took a look around. Eugene Sawyer observed in his book that Gonzalez was soon "partially inebriated and would have become totally unfit for business had not Leiva checked him." So far, they had followed Vasquez' orders to do nothing out of the ordinary until he arrived. Then, however, Moreno showed up and--according to Greenwood--saw proprietor Andrew Snyder paying some money to a man outside. The sight of cash apparently was too much for Moreno. He drew his pistol, promptly ordering Utzerath, Snyder and several customers including a blacksmith named L.C. Smith and Smith's young son to line up against the bar. Leiva and Gonzalez began tying up everyone and forcing them to lie on the floor.

At this point Vasquez arrived with Chavez. He ordered Moreno to stand outside and guard the horses. The first of the three fatal shootings soon took place. The victim was a Portuguese shepherd named Bernal Berhuri, who suddenly appeared in the street and started toward the door. He was ordered to halt, but either did not understand or did not hear. He was shot in the head. Although one account had him killed by Vasquez, it was Moreno who eventually was tried and sentenced for his death.

In the meantime, another young son of blacksmith L.C. Smith walked in and saw what was happening. He dashed out the back door and ran toward the stable. Chavez chased him and, Greenwood wrote, caught him, "knocking him unconscious with his pistol butt." Chavez then dragged the boy back inside and laid him down with the others.

Vasquez stepped outside just as a teamster named George Redford drove up in his wagon with a load of pickets. Vasquez pointed his Henry rifle at Redford and ordered him down. Although Vasquez probably did not know it at the moment, Redford was deaf. Like the Portuguese sheepherder, he did not grasp what he was being told. The teamster quickly noticed the rifle, however, and ran toward the rear of the store. Vasquez shot him as he reached the stable door. The man staggered into the stable and fell on his face in a horse stall. He was dead.

Store owner Andrew Snyder left his own written version of the robbery. It differed in numerous details with the accounts of others. He wrote that he was returning late in the day from the Panoche Valley with his wife, their 3-year-old son and a Mrs. S.L. Moore when he discovered two "well-armed Spaniards" inside the store. A few minutes later, he recalled, "three more Spaniards," also "well-armed," rode up in front, dismounted and entered. Among them was Vasquez himself.

Vasquez laid his hand on Snyder's shoulder, addressed him by name, and asked if there was any mail for him. Snyder said he went behind the Post Office desk to look through the mail only to hear someone say, "Lay down." Snyder turned around and saw his clerk lying down on the floor. Across the room, two of the bandits stood with revolvers cocked. They ordered the store owner to get down on the floor. Another man was in the doorway, his rifle aimed at Snyder. When Snyder did not comply at once, they told him that if he did not obey, they would shoot off the top of his head. He finally lay down, admitting later that it was "the hardest thing to do I ever did in my life." He had an old musket, loaded with buckshot, standing behind the Post Office desk and his first impulse was "to get one or more of them." He quickly thought about his family in the adjoining building, however, and realized that if he tried it, "they in all probability would kill me and my family and Mrs. Moore."

Vasquez came in from the outside and ordered Snyder tied. When Snyder protested, Vasquez said he had "but one way of doing his business" and that was to be "on the safe side." He advised the store owner to submit or be killed. As Snyder recalled, "I then told him that if he would promise me that neither he nor any of his men would go into the rooms where the women were to molest them, I would submit to be tied. They promised me they would not molest the ladies in any way whatsoever." Vasquez tied Snyder's hands securely behind his back, then turned him over on his face and covered him with a blanket. They trussed up the clerk the same way, tying his heels to his hands.

Another man and his wife drove up in front, got out of their wagon and started to enter the store. The man suddenly found a revolver at his head. He was ordered to lie down on the store porch. He did so and was bound. His wife screamed all the time they were tying her husband. Snyder recalled, "They threatened several times to shoot her if she did not stop hollering. At this moment Mrs. Snyder, my wife, stepped out among them and took this lady by the arm and told her to go into her room with her and be quiet and maybe they would not hurt her. She did so. There was one door and one window in the room my wife and child and Mrs. Moore were in, and one of the bandits stood at the open window of this room all the time, with a rifle, on guard."

Just then yet another man, John Haley, arrived in front of the store with a four-horse team. The bandits ordered him to stop and to get down. He refused. One of the gang hit him on the head with a revolver and told him they were robbing the store; that everybody had to obey orders or be killed. Snyder remembered that Haley called to him several times, but "I could not answer him. He finally got down off his wagon and they tied him kneeling down on his knees with his back to the front wheel of his wagon and left him in that position, the horses not tied. Mr. Haley told me afterwards that he had managed to untie his hands from the wheel of the wagon, but remained in the same position until all was over."

Snyder also told of the killing of the third victim:

> ...Mr. Davidson, the man to whom I had rented the hotel...went to the front door of the hotel and opened the door a little to look out to see what was going on. At this time it was getting dark and at this moment Mrs. Davidson, his wife, ran through from the back of the hotel and told him it was robbers and she was just in the act of reaching her arm over his shoulders to close the door. At that moment Vasquez came in front of the door and fired. The ball passed through the door and pierced Mr. Davidson through the heart. He fell dead in his wife's arms.

Although it appears that Vasquez killed both teamster Redford and hotel operator Davidson, it was for the murder of the latter that he was eventually tried and convicted. Vasquez, as we have seen, blamed Leiva for the murders of the sheepherder and the teamster, claiming that it was Romulo Gonzalez who fatally shot Davidson inside the hotel.

Eugene Sawyer's book contained what probably was a fairly accurate account of the killing of Davidson, suggesting that it was caused by the panic of a saddler named Lewis Scherrer, who had been standing in front of the hotel when the bandits first rode up. Apparently thinking nothing of it, Scherrer walked to the rear of the little hotel to wash up, as it was about time for supper.

At this point, Sawyer wrote, E.S. Burton, brother-in-law of Davidson, came in from the stable and saw Vasquez kill Redford as the latter was running toward the stable. Burton shouted to Scherrer, who quickly started running toward his saddle shop adjoining the stable. Vasquez saw him and, with his rifle still raised, ran to head him off. The saddler saw he couldn't make it, so ran back toward the hotel, pushing the door into the kitchen. He then turned and ran to the front of the hotel, where the door was open. Davidson was standing just inside the door with his wife and Burton. The latter apparently had run inside just ahead of Sherrer to warn the Davidsons. They were looking out toward the stable at the body of Redford.

Leiva came running from the store, calling to the Davidsons, "Shut the door and you won't get hurt. Go in! Go in!" Davidson and his wife were standing on either side of the door, with Scherrer and Burton just behind them. Leiva had hardly got the words out of his mouth before Vasquez rounded the corner of the hotel from the rear and rushed up on the porch. Just as Davidson was closing the door, Vasquez fired his rifle. As Sawyer wrote: "The bullet passed through the door and pierced Davidson's heart. He fell back into the arms of his wife, and in a few minutes breathed his last."

It was never clear why Vasquez fired. Perhaps it was the fact that the door was slamming in his face. Perhaps it was simply to keep them all cowed and out of his way until the gang finished its work in the store.

To return to Andrew Snyder's account:

> Three of the bandits including Vasquez came into the store when Vasquez made quite a speech, saying that he was sorry to trouble us in this way. He said he would rather work hard every day, but if he did so and the people found out who he was, they would hang him. He further stated that he had only one way to make a living and that was by robbing, and as long as other people had any money, he intended to have his share of it if he had to kill a man to get it.

Vasquez may well have thought he was delivering a speech that would make him famous and feared. One can almost see him flourishing the black, red-lined cape around himself as he delivered these words to his captive audience. Snyder went on:

> They then went to plundering our pockets, took all the coin we had in our pockets, and our watches. They then went through the money drawer. They then took me up, one man holding me by my hands and another with a rifle at my ear, ordered me to go to the door of my wife's room with them. I did so and then they ordered my wife to bring out all the money there was in the house. It was kept in a bureau drawer. Mrs. Snyder handed them the drawer with all its contents.
>
> They then took me back towards the store and stopped me and asked me if that was all the money I had on hand. I told them it was. Chavez then wanted to kill me. He told Vasquez that I knew them and would be the cause of their arrest some time. Vasquez told him no, that I had submitted and had been a friend to their people and the first man that undertook to harm me, he would shoot the top of his head off. He then took me back into the store and laid me down on the floor on my back, put a cushion under my head and covered me up with a blanket.

Despite the fact that he had just killed two men and that one of his company had murdered another, here was Vasquez at his gentlemanly best again, showing kindness and consideration for a victim. Snyder complained that his hands were tied so tightly that his arms were swollen all the way to his shoulders. He related that he spoke to Vasquez several times about it. The bandit finally examined the rope, agreed that it was too tight and loosened it. Snyder thanked him.

They got in all, the storekeeper recalled, about $430 in cash and about $1,000 worth of goods. Among other things, they took a suit of clothes and, in the words of writer Beers, "deprived the clerk, John Utzerath, of a valuable gold watch and sleeve buttons."

After they were done plundering the store for valuables, said Snyder, they pulled down a lot of crackers, cheese, oysters and sardines and "ate a regular meal." In the store room there were several 10-gallon kegs of beer belonging to the New Idria Quicksilver Company. They rolled one keg out into the store, tapped it and "had a jolly good time." Snyder, tied on the floor with the other victims, asked Vasquez and his men to hurry "as I had not been to my supper yet." The bandits told him they were hungry and would leave when they had finished eating.

It was while they were eating, said the storekeeper, that a 7-year-old boy, a third son of L.C. Smith, entered the store to tell his father to go to supper. The bandits laid the boy down with the others, but did not tie him. After they finished eating, they went to the stable and brought out 11 horses, leading them to the front of the store and packing several of them with Snyder's merchandise. Then they rode off to the south. They were some distance away, Snyder wrote, when his wife's "fine dappled gray horse" broke free and ran back, putting his head right into the open window of Mrs. Snyder's room. The bandits returned for him and led him away again despite her pleas that the horse was a gift and a pet.

After Vasquez and his men left for good, Snyder said, the 7-year-old boy untied his father, who freed the others. Snyder went to his wife's room and found her alive, then to the adjoining room where Mrs. Davidson was lying on the floor in hysterics alongside of her dead husband.

By daylight, Snyder wrote, several hundred people had gathered. "It was a mournful looking sight to behold," he recalled. "Three dead bodies lying together. Poor Mrs. Davidson. She did take it so hard."

The following fall, Snyder sold his store and took his wife east "as she dreaded so much to stay there after that." It was months, he wrote, before she recovered from the shock.

"And," he added, "we never can forget it."

Chapter 11
OUTRAGE AND SHOCK

Shortly after, two of my party separated from us and remained in the upper counties. Chavez, Leiva and myself traveled south without molestation until we reached Rock Creek.

In all, Vasquez and his men spent more than three hours at Tres Pinos, making certain they got everything valuable. Having packed the stolen horses with provisions from the store, they set off through the darkness along San Benito Creek toward the Pichaco mine. They rode hard in order to put as many miles as possible between themselves and the scene of the killings by daybreak. When some of the horses were spent, they switched to others taken from the stable and kept riding.

Just before dawn, they reached the Hernandez Valley adobe of Lorenzo Vasquez, who was a friend of Tiburcio, but not a relative. They had traveled about 50 miles from Snyder's store. Before eating breakfast, Tiburcio divided the loot. He, of course, took the biggest share, including the watch. He was the captain, after all. And, as he explained to his men, things would go hardest with him in the event of capture.

Teodoro Moreno, perhaps feeling that the life of a bandit was not as profitable as he had thought, rode off to a ranch in Bitter Water Valley and went back to shearing sheep for a living. The law, however, was to catch up with him directly.

In the meantime, the people of California were learning about the raid and the hunt for Vasquez was on. Not much of the information reaching print was very accurate. *The Salinas Index* ran the following story on Sept. 4, 1873:

> The brief notice of the telegraphic report of the Tres Pinos murder and robbery which came to hand as we were going to press last week has been too truly verified, and the public have been fully acquainted with the particulars of the outrage by a party of eight desperados, the leaders of whom are well known in this country, where they have been committing their depredations for a number of years, avoiding capture by resorting to the many inaccessible canyons and hiding places which abound in the various mountain ranges.

The newspaper based its story on information from the sheriffs of San Benito and Monterey Counties, both of whom reached the scene the next day. It said the robbery was conducted by "the notorious Tiburcio Vasquez" and noted that he and his men were unmasked, "which fact corroborates the theory that robbery and not murder was the original intention." During the whole business, the newspaper reported, "while the shooting was going on outside, it is said that Vasquez paid no attention to it, busying himself with search for money and plunder."

That, of course, did not jibe with other versions, which laid two of the killings to the bandit leader. Nor did the *The Index's* information that the shooting was all done by one man, José Chabo, "who first shot a Portuguese teamster, who was engaged in greasing his wagon wheels, and who, it is supposed, did not hear and immediately obey an order to lie down."

Where *The Index* even got the name "José Chabo" is a mystery.

The paper said the robbers went through the store, the adjoining rooms and the pockets of their captives, while "the terrified inhabitants," offering no resistance, seemed paralyzed with fear. Eight of the best horses in the stables and on the premises, together with saddles, the *Index* noted, were then taken by the bandits as they lit out for the south.

The newspaper's outraged editor could not resist a little editorializing:

> If the citizens in that locality had acted with sufficient energy and promptness, and had followed the band at once, forcing every man they came across to arm and join the pursuit, a force of at least fifty men would have been on the trail in a few hours, the band would have been killed or taken, together with the stock and plunder; but the inhabitants were terror-stricken and entertained fears of a subsequent visit and revenge by the terrible Vasquez if they even attempted their own protection.

While the newspaper said eight bandits took part in the raid, most accounts indicated there were only five or six. Tiburcio Vasquez himself, in his later Los Angeles jail cell interview with *The Daily Herald*, stated that he had only four men with him, identifying them as Chavez, Leiva and "two friends of Leiva." He made no mention of Romulo Gonzalez or of Teodoro Moreno. By the time of the interview, the latter already was under arrest for the murder of the Portuguese sheepherder.

In that interview, Vasquez claimed that he and Chavez rode to the store to discover "the men tied and the murders already committed. I scolded the men for disobeying my orders and said, 'Let's all leave.' I said to the lady whose husband was tied that if she did not give me the money I would kill him. She gave me the money. I did not kill him."

As Greenwood wrote, news of the Tres Pinos tragedy "outraged and shocked the public and many local communities feared an imminent attack from the Vasquez banditti." Some newspaper accounts, he said, suggested that Vasquez had as many as 50 men under arms, divided into bands and "all working under his evil genius."

Joseph Henry Jackson, in his book *Bad Company,* about the bandits of early California, wrote, "The news of the Tres Pinos tragedy horrified the public, and fresh efforts were made to capture Vasquez. For a month or two there was a great amateur riding up and down in the Coast Range and the San Joaquin Valley. All that the posses found was a dead campfire here or an abandoned horse and some clothing in another place..."

Panic certainly swept the town of Hollister, a dozen miles north of Snyder's store. Residents there apparently expected Vasquez to come swooping down upon them within a few hours. Vigilantes gathered with their guns and were posted on all the roads to watch for the murderous bandits.

In its 1927 feature on the life of Vasquez, *The Hollister Evening Free Lance* told of one of the vigilantes, J.G. Hamilton, whose first night on duty found him lying behind the corral fence at the Eagle stables, "gun in hand and straining his eyes through the darkness with the expectation any minute of seeing Vasquez and his gang, armed to the teeth, and marching on a slumbering Hollister, while at home his newly wedded bride had visions of her young husband meeting with a tragic end at the hands of the outlaw gang."

As the night wore on, the newspaper said, "the air grew chill and no outlaws hove into sight. Hamilton gradually lost his enthusiasm for guard duty and finally, a while before daylight came, he sneaked away home. Afterward he learned that he had not been the only committeeman to decide that there were plenty of others on the job in case Vasquez did come. He often wondered if a single guardsman would have been on the job to protect the populace if the outlaw had ridden in just before dawn.

Apparently the town stayed on edge for a week or two. According to one version, Hollister first got word of the attack from one of its citizens, Johnnie Zumwalt, who happened to be at Tres Pinos when the shooting broke out. He managed to sneak away and walk the dozen miles to Hollister, staying off the road in case Vasquez and his men came riding north on their getaway.

In addition, an itinerant chicken-and-egg man named Campbell and his young son purportedly were unhitching their horses in the barn behind Snyder's store at the time of the raid. It was said they, too, slipped away and walked for several miles, finally getting a ride to Hollister with a passing teamster.

Dominga Hoffer said in her book that she was told by the store clerk, Utzerath, that all the victims lay tied for an hour after the gang left them, and that at last he called out to Johnny Smith, the blacksmith's son, "Get the cheese knife from the counter and cut us loose." By Utzerath's account, a Chinese cook and the egg man, Campbell, who had fled when he first saw Vasquez' men approaching, finally went to the neighboring ranches to report the news. The store clerk claimed that the Chinese cook ran around shouting, "Fire! Fire! Shoot! Shoot! Two bosses killed! Dead!"

Utzerath said that he, after being cut loose, walked to the nearby McPhail ranch, where he borrowed a horse and rode along the foothills away from the road until he reached Hollister. By that time, he said, it was so late at night that there was only one saloon open. He and the saloon keeper "spread the alarm." Young Dan McPhail also rode into Hollister, said Hoffer, but it is unclear whether he arrived there before Utzerath.

From reading the various accounts, it seems that half the people who were in Tres Pinos on that bloody evening were trying to take credit for notifying the rest of the state.

Utzerath told Hoffer that he went before the justice of the peace in Hollister and swore out a warrant for the arrest of Teodoro Moreno, Vasquez' cousin. Why he didn't swear one out for Vasquez himself, he did not say. Perhaps he was unaware at the time that Vasquez apparently killed Redford and Davidson. Possibly he was certain only of the fact that Moreno killed the Portuguese sheepherder, Bernal Berhuri.

Utzerath, who may have built up his own role a bit in his talk with Dominga Hoffer, said he then went to the Southern Pacific Railroad telegraphic operator and sent a message about the raid to *The San Francisco Chronicle*. That account, published by *The Chronicle* on the morning of August 28, was in Hoffer's words, "the first news given to the outside world."

The warrant was served on Moreno a short time later as he sheared sheep on the ranch in Bitter Water Valley.

(According to both Beers and Greenwood, Moreno was not arrested until after Abdon Leiva turned himself in and told the lawmen where to find him, but as Moreno was already convicted for the murder of Berhuri by the time Vasquez went to court, it is probable the sheep shearer was taken into custody prior to Leiva's surrender.)

No matter who properly gets the credit for being the first to spread the news of the events at Snyder's store, another of the McPhail family had a good deal to do with eventually sending Tiburcio Vasquez to the gallows. He was D.F.H. McPhail, who may have been the father of Dan. He had been in Hollister that day and was returning to Tres Pinos on the stage early that evening. He got off the stage near Snyder's stable and was walking toward his ranch a half mile away just as Vasquez and Cleovaro Chavez rode in the direction of the store, where Leiva, Gonzalez and Moreno were already at work. As Vasquez and Chavez came across

McPhail, they saw that he was wearing a heavy gold chain, which suggested a good-sized watch in his vest pocket. Chavez dismounted and asked McPhail what time it was.

McPhail pulled out the watch and Chavez reached to grab it, but then hesitated and looked back at Vasquez. The latter shook his head no. McPhail told them the time and put his watch away. Vasquez said politely, "Thank you, *Señor*." He then asked whether that was Andrew Snyder's store just ahead, as though he did not know. McPhail told him it was and they took their leave politely.

Vasquez was to learn later that McPhail had returned from Hollister with $500 in cash and a check for another $200. He probably regretted that he had not robbed him. More than that, he had cause to wish he had eliminated the man altogether. McPhail's testimony, placing Vasquez on the approach to Snyder's store just before the fatal shootings, was to be very damaging to the bandit chieftan at his murder trial.

After the raid Vasquez headed south with Chavez, Leiva and Gonzalez into Kern County. That required more than 150 miles of hard riding, mostly through hills of scrub oak and the flat Central Valley, until they reached desert country. They stopped to rest their horses as seldom as possible because the posses were looking for them. In three days they reached Buena Vista Lake near Bakersfield, where Gonzalez parted company with them, apparently because his horse gave out. Vasquez, Leiva and Chavez went on to the little settlement of San Emedio, where Joaquin Castro's son was waiting for them with Rosario and the children.

As for Rosario, she was waiting for Tiburcio Vasquez.

He did not stay with her immediately, however, feeling it would be dangerous for all of them to travel together while the posses were stirring. He rode on ahead with Chavez into Los Angeles County, leaving Abdon Leiva to bring the family. As Vasquez rode through Tejon Pass to Elizabeth Lake, Chavez waited for the Leivas at a ranch near Fort Tejon so he could guide them to rejoin Tiburcio. They met at Elizabeth Lake, where they camped for a couple of days, then rode to Jim Heffner's ranch in the foothills overlooking the Antelope Valley, where Rosario and the children were to stay. As it turned out, only the children remained there. Rosario, desperate not to let Vasquez out of her sight again, found a woman to take care of them and chose to ride with her husband and her lover to camp in Little Rock Creek Canyon over the San Bernardino County line.

Abdon Leiva was sick of the outlaw life, of hiding from *gringo* posses and sleeping among the cold rocks with gritty wind snuffing out his cooking fire, but Rosario seemed to love it.

Or, at least, she loved Vasquez.

Tiburcio Vasquez on the day before he was executed

Tiburcio Vasquez at 18

--California Collection
California state Library

Abdon Leiva

--San Jose Historical Museum

Juan Soto
"The Human Wildcat"
--Wells Fargo Bank

Tomas Redundo
alias Procopio
--San Jose Historical Museum

Alameda County Sheriff
Harry N. Morse
--Wells Fargo Bank

Santa Clara County Sheriff
John Adams
--San Jose Historical Museum

Harry Morse (seated far right) after he became a detective for Wells Fargo & Co. Others: Railroad detective Stone (top left), Wells Fargo detective John Thacker (top right), San Joaquin County Sheriff Thomas Cunningham (left front) and Calaveras County Sheriff Ben Thron.
--Wells Fargo Bank

Vasquez Rocks in Los Angeles County--one of Tiburcio's favorite hideouts

Elizabeth Lake. Another Los Angeles County stomping ground for Vasquez

The one-time home of Tiburcio Vasquez' sister Dolores was bought by Monterey as an art center in 1949. Vasquez hid out there now and then--although it was only a block from the jail. It originally was a one-story adobe.

San Jose, Diciembre 11 de 1874
Sr. Don Charles B. Darwin
Muy Señor Mio
Siendo vd. el Abogado principal que esta
encargado de hacer mi defensa razon por
la cual es mi deber el poner en su
conocimiento de vd. que yo estoy en el
mayor peligro de ser sacrificado y si
a vd. le puede mi situacion segun yo
le manifiesto a vd. entonces yo espero en la
bondad de vd. sedignara el venir para
hacerle yo una explicacion exacta sobre
de mi situacion. sirvase Sr. el dispensarme
esta molestia y al mismo tiempo Considerarme
Renuevo a vd. mi alta
Consideracion y particular
Aprecio Tiburcio Vasquez

In his beautiful handwriting, Vasquez wrote to attorney Charles B. Darwin while awaiting trial in San Jose. He wished to explain the danger he was in.

--The Huntington, San Marino, Calif.

A mi idolatrado hijo.
El dia de su Cumpleaños

oh rodolfo bendito este dia
En que hermoso te miro crecer.
En que un angel me dice has de ser
En la tierra mi bien mi alegria.

Con dolor que mi pecho taladre
Deja bese tu frente de niño
Recibiendo el inmenso cariño
Que ahora y siempre te tiene tu padre

Eres tu, de mi amor el tesoro.
un recuerdo feliz de ventura
Hoy no mas con tu amante ternura
Calmar puedes mi ferviente lloro

Con tu amor tu sostienes mi vida
y al fulgor de tus candidos ojos
No tropieza mi planta entre abrojos
y por ti la existencia es querida

Hoy al verte tan bello hijo mio
Te bendigo con santo embeleso.
y te abrazo rodolfo y te beso
y al mirarte feliz me extasio.
Tiburcio Vasquez,

Birthday letter from Vasquez to his son, Rodolfo. Date unknown.
--California Section
California State Library

SHERIFF'S OFFICE,
County of Santa Clara.

San Jose, March .... 1875.

To ....

SIR.—Pursuant to the Statute in such cases you are hereby invited to be present at the execution of Tiburcio Vasquez, at the Jail of said County, in San Jose, on the 19th day of March, A. D. 1875, at 1:30 o'clock P. M.

J. H. ADAMS, Sheriff.

PRESENT AT JAIL ENTRANCE. NOT TRANSFERABLE.

FACSIMILE

Invitation to a hanging.

Chapter 12
CAUGHT IN THE ACT

I seduced the wife of the man Leiva. He did not discover our intimacy until we had pitched camp at the lake. He at once rebelled and swore revenge.

All the time Tiburcio Vasquez was moving down to Southern California after the murderous raid on Snyder's store, Sheriff John H. Adams of Santa Clara County was after him. The sheriff had been in Gilroy campaigning for re-election when he heard of the robbery the next morning. He recognized the vote-getting value of a dramatic pursuit, caught a freight train that was headed for Hollister and was there by 10 a.m. He immediately set about to organize a posse.

That, however, was not so easy. The word around the countryside was that Vasquez had a band of 15 to 20 men--perhaps more--heavily armed and ready to kill. Adams telegraphed Sheriff Tom Wasson of Monterey County, who arrived about 3 p.m. The two of them managed to recruit only six or seven men willing to ride after Vasquez. By this time, Adams was sorry he had not started in pursuit alone, because almost an entire day had been lost. The posse did not set out until late afternoon on the day after the raid. Several other men joined the group on the way to Tres Pinos. As they rode up Tres Pinos Creek, they were far behind.

The posse members learned that the bandits had paused at Lorenzo Vasquez' ranch to divide the loot, but Lorenzo denied it absolutely. The posse then tracked the fugitives as far as the Hernandez Valley, but lost the scent. They went over a steep trail into Cantua Canyon, Tiburcio's old hideout, where they were told by a sheepherder that the bandits had passed through without stopping.

It was not until August 29, three days after the Los Pinos raid, that the posse reached Baker's Ranch in Pleasant Valley. There, they found tracks that pointed to Tulare Lake in Kern County--where they once again lost the trail and finally straggled into Fresno. Sheriff Wasson didn't know the countryside, so he decided to go back to Monterey County and organize another posse that would make a further search of the La Cantua area. Meanwhile, Santa Clara County Sheriff Adams telegraphed the sheriff of Kern County to get some men together and wait for him.

When he arrived in Bakersfield, Adams found a grand total of two Kern County deputies at his disposal. The three of them rode toward Tejon Pass. It is not known what happened to the other original members of the Adams posse, but it is probable they wearied of the chase and went home. At Buena Vista Lake, Adams stopped to question a Mexican sleeping beside the trail. The man said he knew nothing and had not seen anybody resembling Tiburcio Vasquez. That man, as Adams later learned with what reporter George Beers described as "considerable chagrin," was Romulo Gonzalez, who had just left Vasquez, Chavez and Leiva at the lake. Vasquez subsequently accused Gonzalez of killing Leander Davidson. Adams had no description of Gonzalez, so did not recognize him. The sheriff found a new coat and new pair of pants in a sack Gonzalez carried, but the latter claimed they were his Sunday clothes. It is likely they were taken from Snyder's store.

Even if the man had been arrested, Adams pointed out after he discovered his error, there was not at that time a jail in Bakersfield and no way to take him into custody without delaying the pursuit of Tiburcio Vasquez. It was generally assumed that Gonzalez then fled to Mexico--Sunday clothes and all.

Adams and his posse came across the tracks of Vasquez, Chavez and Leiva somewhere south of Buena Vista Lake and followed the trail to San Emedio, where a blacksmith said he had shod two sorrels brought in by Vasquez and Chavez.

Like everything else printed on the subject, the story of Sheriff Adams' pursuit is muddled by the disagreement among various writers. It only seems clear that Adams found his way to Heffner's ranch near Lake Elizabeth in northern Los Angeles County. Whether he was aware that Leiva's two children were there, no one knows, but he apparently learned that a wagon matching the description of the one being used by Leiva to transport his family had passed there the day before. He was too late, however, to catch the three bandits. By that time, they were camping with Rosario at Little Rock Creek Canyon in the boulder-strewn foothills southeast of the present-day Antelope Valley city of Palmdale.

Not finding Vasquez, Chavez and Leiva at Heffner's, Adams rode alone to Tejon Pass and sent a telegram to Sheriff William Rowland of Los Angeles County, saying that Vasquez was almost certainly somewhere in the area and asking that Rowland join forces with him in the search. Adams then rode back to a spot near Heffner's ranch, where he waited for Rowland.

Two days later, the Los Angeles County sheriff arrived with six men and an Indian guide. Rowland apparently also had a tip that Vasquez and his friends were camping in Little Rock Creek Canyon, where they were drying stolen beef in preparation for what the lawmen assumed was a planned escape to Mexico. Rowland and Adams led their posse to the mouth of the canyon, where they found some fresh wagon tracks. They rode up into the canyon and discovered a cache of food as well as the cold remains of campfires. Hanging from the limbs of a tree were three quarters of a large beef, cut into chunks.

The two sheriffs decided to ride farther up into the canyon in an effort to surprise Vasquez and his companions. The canyon was a narrow, twisting one with steep, rocky sides. There were scrub trees, cactus and stretches of deep sand. It wasn't long before they saw a man ride into view from behind a clump of manzanita. He was Chavez. One foolish deputy shouted, "There's a man!" Chavez heard this and spurred his horse up a ravine. Moments later, he had vanished. Because his horse was fresher, he had no trouble outdistancing his pursuers. Adams, Rowland and the posse rode after him, shooting blindly in their excitement. They soon found themselves at a puzzling fork in the trail.

Chavez and Vasquez suddenly began firing their Henry rifles at the lawmen from a high boulder. The posse scattered.

After he and his men had retreated to safety, Adams wanted to charge after the fugitives again, but Rowland argued that they should wait for the posse members to regroup. That left Adams to pursue Vasquez and Chavez alone. The bandits had stopped firing, so Adams remounted and rode back up the canyon, convinced that they were escaping. He was right. As he reached the top of the canyon, he saw the pair disappearing into the chaparral. By the time Rowland and the other posse members joined Adams, the bandits were gone. Although they failed to catch Vasquez and Chavez, the sheriffs reportedly found nine horses, some of which matched the descriptions of those taken from Snyder's stable in Tres Pinos. The posse led the horses back to Tejon Pass.

Leiva, who had not liked the lawless life to begin with, was by now thoroughly disenchanted. He apparently was afraid that he would hang for his part in the Tres Pinos raid. The fact that he was Chilean would not help, he knew. To the *gringos* he was just another "greaser." In addition, he must have known by this time that Rosario and Vasquez were more than friends. It was this, more than anything, that prompted him to turn on his old captain.

As Vasquez was to tell the editor of *The Los Angeles Star*, "A criminal intimacy had existed between myself and Leiva's wife long before I left the ranch in Monterey County. But Leiva never suspected us. At Rock Creek he caught us *in fragrante delicto*. He turned against me then, and sought to have me captured."

It was shortly after Sheriffs Adams and Rowland lost Vasquez and Chavez in the canyon that Leiva became a traitor. The three bandits and Rosario were camped among the rocks and were getting low on food. Vasquez told Leiva to take the wagon to Heffner's ranch and bring back some provisions. Leiva said he would return about midnight. He returned several hours before that, however, and discovered Vasquez entwined with Rosario beneath a blanket. That did not please him. Reporter George Beers, some of whose lurid fiction we have already read, described the scene improbably as follows:

> The infuriated husband, with a dramatic air, drew a pistol from his pocket, when Chavez, whose manner of life had rendered him extremely wakeful, sprang, pantherlike, from his warm nest and, covering Leiva with his Dragon pistol, exclaimed, "If you fire I will blow your brains out!"
>
> Leiva weakened at once, put up his pistol, but said to Vasquez, "Be sure I will kill you if I get a chance." And then he expressed a willingness to fight a "fair" duel, Chavez to act as second. Meanwhile, the unfortunate woman was sitting up in bed, her face covered by her hands and weeping bitterly.
>
> To Leiva's proposition, Vasquez returned a singular and very diplomatic answer. "No, Leiva," replied the hunted bandit. "I do not wish to add to the wrong I have already done you. I will not fight with you except compelled to. You have no right to risk depriving your children of a protector. You have a right to seek revenge if you think proper, and then I shall be justified in defending myself."

> After some further conversation, an understanding was had that no hostilities should take place until they had separated. After that event, Leiva warned him he should attack him whenever and wherever they met. Next morning, Leiva parted from them, leaving his wife and children at Jim Heffner's, saying that he would "shirk for myself."

Whether Leiva divulged to Rosario his plan to give himself up and bring about the capture of Vasquez is unknown. He left her with their children at Heffner's ranch and rode off alone on horseback. He went to Lyon's Station, where he found a Los Angeles County deputy sheriff named W.W. Jenkins. Leiva promptly identified himself and offered to help lawmen find Tiburcio Vasquez.

Vasquez was not long in hearing about Levia's treachery. A *Californio* who had himself been hiding out at Heffner's rode to Little Rock Creek Canyon to tell the bandit. Vasquez was furious. He mounted his palomino and went toward Lake Elizabeth through the rocks and canyons, avoiding trails where he might encounter Sheriffs Adams and Rowland or any of their deputies.

Vasquez arrived at Heffner's in the darkness, quickly found Rosario and took her away. She was later to claim that she was abducted at gunpoint, but that accusation was made after Vasquez apparently abandoned her in the hills. She was to testify against him at his trial, offering a picture far different from the one she might have painted at the height of her infatuation for him.

In the meantime, the *yanqui* lawmen had not only found the horses apparently stolen from Snyder's stable, they had discovered an adobe where Vasquez and his friends had stashed a saddle and some clothing--all identifiable as having been taken from Snyder's store. At yet another house, they found several *Mexicanos* who had befriended Vasquez and who were keeping two trunks he left there. In the trunks were clothing and jewelry, said to have been stolen at Tres Pinos.

By the following morning, the posse arrived at Heffner's ranch, having been told by some residents of the area that Leiva was seen taking his wife there. When they arrived, they saw what they believed to be Leiva's wagon sitting outside a small adobe. They approached carefully, immediately dispatching one of their number to talk to Heffner himself. Heffner said Leiva was not there. Nor, he said, was Rosario. He said "a man" had taken her away during the night. The posse wanted to know why he hadn't prevented it. Heffner told them that several of Vasquez' men were believed to be in the vicinity and he was afraid to interfere.

At this point, the posse members encountered Deputy Sheriff Jenkins and his prisoner, the suddenly talkative Abdon Leiva. Informed of the location of Vasquez' camp, some of the posse members headed for Little Rock Creek Canyon. Sheriff Adams, who was just about worn out by then, decided to return to Monterey County and to look for Moreno and Gonzalez in that area, to which some believed they had returned.

The attack on Snyder's store at Tres Pinos had created much excitement throughout California. Newspapers began to attribute almost any robbery anywhere to Tiburcio Vasquez and his band. It was widely believed by *gringos*--and by many *Californios*--that he already had a large army in the saddle and was constantly on the move. The name of Tiburcio Vasquez was well known at last. He might have been amused to read in Beers' book about the atmosphere that prevailed:

> The people in Southern California were especially exposed to the depredations of the desperadoes, and kept in continual alarm; and Los Angeles, where the wonderful fertility of soil, exquisite beauty of scenery, and health-giving climate was attracting the attention of Eastern capitalists, tourists and people throughout the East desirous of locating there--suffered greatly from the fact that the continued depredations of these

> bandits created such a general alarm as to turn the tide of travel in other directions. It is a fact well known that hundreds of people who left their business in the East and came to California for the express purpose of visiting Los Angeles and other portions of Southern California, on reaching Sacramento, and finding in the morning papers accounts of the daring operations of Vasquez, introduced with horrible headlines, and graphically written up, actually stopped short in their journey, not daring to risk their lives and property by traveling through the regions in which the bold outlaws operated--and returned to their Eastern homes, where they could rest in comparative safety.

Although he was hiding out in the rocky hills of Southern California, Vasquez obviously kept up on what was going on. News was relayed to him by admiring *Mexicanos*. No doubt he had heard that his cousin, Teodoro Moreno, shearing sheep in Bitter Water Valley, had been taken to jail in Salinas, where he was soon joined by Leiva. Both were indicted for their parts in the Tres Pinos raid. Perhaps because of threats by Moreno, Leiva was transferred to the Santa Clara County jail at San Jose.

Beers reported on Moreno's trial in *The San Francisco Chronicle*:

> The courtroom was densely thronged throughout the trial. The first witness introduced by the prosecution was the "reformed" bandit, Abdon Leiva, who gave a clear and succinct account of each event in the Tres Pinos tragedy. A rigid cross-examination failed to elicit a single lame point in his straight-forward story. His story was corroborated by his wife, as far as her knowledge of the plotting of the robbery and the subsequent event.

Moreno's defense consisted of testimony by Manuel Larios, Vasquez' brother-in-law, and by one Concepción Espinoza,* whom Beers termed "a woman of doubtful character" trying to provide the defendant with an alibi.

Moreno denied on the stand that he had been part of the Tres Pinos raiding party. He said he had been busy at the time with trying to find a lost horse. Moreno testified that he had encountered Vasquez, Chavez, Gonzalez and Leiva having breakfast at Lorenzo Vasquez' house the morning before the robbery, but that he left to shear sheep at a nearby ranch and "was not present at a plot made at Leiva's house to rob Snyder's store." As for the evening of the crime, he claimed, he was with Concepción Espinoza, but "I did not stay there all night." He said he left the lady about 2 or 3 o'clock in the morning.

On cross-examination, observed Beers, Moreno was "inextricably entangled in the thread of his narration...and so confused that it was evident that he was dealing in fiction."

Moreno was found guilty of the murder of Bernal Berhuri, the Portuguese sheepherder, and was sentenced to life in prison. Moreno, according to one reporter who interviewed him, was happy enough not to hang.

In the meantime, after several weeks of hiding in the hills of Southern California, Vasquez apparently decided to ride with Chavez toward his old haunts around Cantua Canyon and New Idria. There was one problem: Rosario.

Here, once again, the writers offered widely divergent ac-

**Although Beers did not mention it and although he spelled the name* Espinoza, *it is probable that this was the same Concepción Espinosa who was a niece of Vasquez and who had lived in Benito with saloon keeper José Castro, lynched for helping the bandit rob a stagecoach.*

counts of Vasquez' final separation from his paramour. Beers wrote that Vasquez gave her money to return to her friends and that he even "devised a fictitious story for her to make public."

Greenwood concluded that "when her presence became an impediment to Vasquez' plans to move north again, he abandoned her in the mountains. Eventually, she made her way to San Jose."

Sawyer wrote:

> At last Vasquez, being afraid that he would be captured if he kept the woman with him, one day left her alone in the hills far away from any settlement, and started northward. Mrs. Leiva was then pregnant, and her sufferings for several days, until she reached the house of a kind farmer, can better be imagined than described. She eventually made her way to San Jose. The children had previously been placed in trustworthy hands at Los Angeles by her husband.

Vasquez may have wondered what she expected of him. How, he might have asked, could a pregnant woman ride with him as he stayed ahead of lawmen in the rocky canyons? By the time she was interviewed in San Jose by a *San Francisco Chronicle* reporter, she had nothing kind to say about Vasquez. According to the newspaper, here is how Rosario Leiva described her departure with the bandit from Heffner's ranch:

> About the middle of the night Vasquez came to the house. The first intimation I had that he was about was when he put his hand on my shoulder and awakened me. I was lying in bed. He had one hand on my shoulder and (in) the other he held a pistol, which was cocked and pointed towards me. He told me to get up quick and go with him, or he would blow my brains

> out. I asked him what I could do with my children. He said he didn't care anything about them.
>
> I did not get up at the first time he told me to, and he came back to the bed again and said if I didn't jump out of bed he would kill me. I was afraid he would do it, so I got up. He ordered me to get on my clothes and go with him as soon as possible. I was crying all the time I was dressing. He put me up on his horse and got up behind me, and started for the Cheviral Mountains.

They were in the mountains for eight days, Rosario told *The Chronicle*, during which she was crying a good deal of the time. Vasquez became very angry with her for that, she recalled. She said she was three or four months pregnant and her health was failing rapidly because of the exposure and ill treatment. She had a miscarriage. Vasquez, she said, then rode off with Chavez, leaving her "sick, helpless and alone." She said he told her, "You can get out of here the best way you can with God's help."

She said she started walking down the mountain toward the valley, and just before dark came to the tent of an old *Americano* sheepherder. He gave her some coffee and bread and allowed her to stay for the night. As he spoke no Spanish and she did not speak English, they had difficulty communicating. It was the first time she had been in a bed for nearly two weeks, she recalled.

The next morning, she told the newspaper, the shepherd gave her a good breakfast and she set out to find some house where she could be taken care of, "as I was very sick." Finally, she said, a Mexican on horseback found her. She told him who she was and what had happened. He put her on his horse and took her to his house "where I was kindly taken care of during my sickness." When they thought her strong enough to stand the journey, she said, the man and his wife took her to the railroad station and paid her passage to San Jose.

Vasquez, no doubt, would have preferred the kinder, gentler version presented by Dominga Hoffer, who suggested that Rosario had gone willingly with Vasquez from Heffner's ranch and that in the early days after riding off together they planned to lie quiet for a few months, then escape to Mexico. The physical discomfort of living in the hills, said Hoffer, meant nothing to them. "Though they were reduced to almost Indian simplicity of life and they had to endure many hardships," Hoffer related, neither complained. "To the lovers those were perfect days. They lived each day as if it were their last. Calmly, they seemed to walk hand in hand with death. They were exalted and purified by its presence. Death was never far away from the fugitives."

Just where Hoffer got such stuff is not known. Certainly it was not the way Rosario told it.

For several weeks in the autumn of 1873, Hoffer wrote, Rosario, Vasquez and the ever-present Cleovaro Chavez lived in the mountains of San Bernardino County, finding shelter in huts or tents, but never staying long in any one location. In Hoffer's version, Rosario gave birth to a premature baby fathered by Vasquez. She and the bandit supposedly wrapped the child in a blanket and Vasquez set out to find clothing for it. Chavez, said the author, remained to care for Rosario. Vasquez allegedly rode down into the valley where he waylaid a peddler and relieved him of clothes for the child. For a few days, Hoffer wrote, "the son of Rosario and Vasquez lived in a kind of stupor. The mother could not be moved and so for a time the group risked capture. Chavez was uneasy, but Vasquez seemed not to care. He felt that should he be obliged to surrender on account of the child of Rosario and himself, it would be worth the risk."

One suspects Hoffer was being especially fanciful when she wrote that Vasquez ventured forth to find a priest when it was clear the baby was near death. As the child lay dying, Hoffer wrote, Rosario began weeping and moaning over the fact that he had never been baptized. The imaginative Hoffer wrote that Vasquez found a Spanish-speaking priest and brought him back into the mountains where the bandit confessed that he was Tiburcio Vasquez. The priest said the secret was safe with him. The priest supposedly advised, “You should send the poor, unhappy woman back to her children and her husband.”

To which Tiburcio Vasquez purportedly replied, “Perhaps. But, Father, even our misery together has great beauty. We never know what is going to happen. We understand the great uncertainty and peril. We hope to escape to Mexico. We are willing to risk everything for happiness.”

Then, if Hoffer is to be believed, the baby died in Rosario’s arms. Chavez supposedly rode out for supplies and returned to the camp with a Los Angeles newspaper from which Vasquez learned that Leiva had testified against Teodoro Moreno in Salinas and had said Tiburcio was the “real culprit” in the murders at Tres Pinos. The same paper reported that Moreno had been convicted and sentenced to prison for life.

Also, to listen to Hoffer, Rosario sobbed that she was holding Vasquez and Chavez back; that if it were not for her, the two could ride out of the area, away from the *gringo* lawmen who were still hunting them. Hoffer wrote:

> “Go,” she said. “See if you can’t find a place where you can leave me.”
>
> Vasquez was moved by the pain in her face. “Don’t worry, probecita. We’ll stay till you are well enough to go.”
>
> “Meanwhile, a sheriff will find us,” Chavez said. “It’s liable to happen any day.”
>
> Rosario sobbed in Vasquez’s arms. “Leave me behind. Go!”
>
> Vasquez held her close. “Never shall we go without you, pobrecita! You have been too brave.”

"Rosario," said Chavez, "every day brings us closer to the gallows. We must leave."

"You go, Cleovaro," suggested Vasquez. "I'll stay here."

Dominga Hoffer's version was that Vasquez and Chavez planned to make one more big raid up north, then return to Rosario so they could all go to Mexico together. While Chavez went to Los Angeles to recruit some men, Hoffer said, Vasquez remained with Rosario for a few more days before parting from her. Apparently her frazzled appearance excited him:

> Never in her voluptuous young strength had Rosario been so appealing as (when she) was wasted and weak... Rosario's illness had softened and refined his feeling. He suffered that he must be separated from her for even a brief time. They told each other that it was for only a few weeks. They clung together as they sobbed their parting words of love. They promised each other that when again they came together there should be no other separation. But this was only a mirage of love that gave them strength for leave-taking. For the last time they melted together in embrace. When next they met, Vasquez was in jail in San Jose.

And Rosario was saying some very unpleasant things about him.

Chapter 13
THE KINGSTON RAID

After sending Leiva's wife home, I went to Kings River in Tulare County, where with a party of eight men besides myself, I captured and tied up 35 men.

Although the jailhouse statement Vasquez made to *Los Angeles Star* editor Ben Truman seems reasonably accurate, the bandit appears to have had two of his raids confused during the interview. He told Truman that he left Rosario "at a sheep ranch while I went on and made a raid at Firebaugh's Ferry on the San Joaquin River for money to send her back to her parents' house. I did so and have not seen her since. I provided for all her wants while she was with me. I tied ten men and a Chinaman at Firebaugh's Ferry, in the raid above referred to."

The Firebaugh's Ferry raid, however, had occurred in the spring of 1873--several months prior to the bloody attack on Snyder's Store at Tres Pinos. It was only after the latter event that Vasquez fled to Southern California and carried on further with Rosario. It wasn't until December of that year--after he had rid himself of the unhappy lady--that Vasquez and his gang swept down upon the little town of Kingston on the Kings River near Fresno, where they indeed took over the whole town and tied up a lot of men--including one of Asian descent.

Editor Truman does not seem to have asked Vasquez about the apparent discrepancy. It is little wonder that the accounts of the career of Tiburcio Vasquez all are as vague as a Spanish land grant.

In any event, with Rosario no longer hindering his actions, Vasquez decided it was time to begin assembling some reliable men and to move north again in order to make some profitable raids. He may still have had it in mind to make his way to Mexico, where he might raise a small army and drive back into California. But he probably suspected that Sheriff Rowland of Los Angeles County was watching all the passes to the south and--for all he knew--had some *Mexicanos* who would be willing for a few *yanqui* dollars to report his presence to the law if he showed up in the proximity of some rancho.

Because Cleovaro Chavez had not served time in prison, Vasquez concluded that he would not be as quickly identified and that it would be easy enough for him to ride to Los Angeles and try to learn what was happening. While there, Chavez was also to see whether he could recruit some men. Vasquez waited in the mountains while Chavez rode by night to the adobe of George Allen near Cahuenga Pass. Greek George, as he was known, was--like Jim Heffner--a *gringo* who had no use for the law and who could be counted on to provide a hiding place. For a price. There, Chavez left his rifle and the sorrel that had been taken from Snyder's store at Tres Pinos. He feared that the latter would be recognized by some sharp-eyed deputy. Borrowing another horse, he rode to Sonora, which was the Mexican district of Los Angeles, and looked up a certain Isadore Padillo, who had been tried for complicity in the murder of an entire family in Tulare County, but had been acquitted because of lack of evidence. Vasquez had told Chavez that Padillo would be a fine man to have in the new regiment and that he could be trusted because he hated the *yanqui* law just as Vasquez and Chavez did.

The idea of riding with Tiburcio Vasquez seemed a good one to Padillo, who was able to tell Chavez that, according to the newspapers, the various posses had pretty well given up the hunt for the bandit leader. Chavez apparently told him that he and Vasquez were planning to help Moreno escape from jail in Salinas, and that appealed to him also.

Before returning to Greek George's with Padillo, Chavez found a *gringo* to rob of a gold watch and about $90. This may have made him feel good about himself again. He and Vasquez had been lying low with Rosario so long that he had probably lost his edge. It probably also enabled him to pay the Greek for his hospitality. Then Chavez took Padillo to San Francisquito Canyon and on to the the rocky foothills where Vasquez waited. Vasquez sent Chavez to Posa de Chane near San Emedio to find all the reliable men he could. Meanwhile, Vasquez told Padillo to ride to the little Mexican settlement of Panama on the Kern River and see whether he could find a fierce man named Gomez, reported to be hiding out after killing a constable trying to serve a warrant on him near Tehachapi. That was the kind of man Vasquez wanted.

Vasquez was soon back in his old hideout at La Cantua Canyon in the Panoche Mountains with Chavez, Padillo, Gomez, a man named Monteres and Blas Bicuna, who had been with him on the futile attempt to derail the Southern Pacific payroll train. There were numerous men in the region who were willing to join Vasquez and he had no trouble gathering a force whenever he needed it. He no doubt meant to make the name Tiburcio Vasquez feared in every *gringo* household from Mexico to the Oregon border, sweeping down out of the canyons once again, striking from the north while the foolish posses sought him in the south.

By now it was October of 1873, two months after his violent attack at Tres Pinos.

Vasquez was still determined to free his cousin, Moreno, from jail. For one thing, neither Chavez nor Vasquez was anxious to have him testify if either was captured. Since Bicuna knew Monterey County, Vasquez dispatched him to Salinas to see what he could find out. Bicuna said he was acquainted with a Mexican woman who would be willing to visit Moreno at the jail and tell him of the captain's plans to free him. When Bicuna returned to the canyon, however, he said Moreno had told the woman it would only make things worse for him if anyone tried to rescue him and failed. He apparently felt there was no chance of such an effort succeeding.

Vasquez could see that Moreno had lost his daring.

The next thing Vasquez had in mind was to find another woman to visit Abdon Leiva in jail in San Jose and take him some enchiladas--the last Leiva would ever eat. Vasquez planned to poison him and make certain he would never testify. Vasquez told Bicuna to do this, but the latter politely declined, saying that he was too well known to Sheriff Adams of Santa Clara County. Gomez, too, did not want to take on the job of providing Leiva with his last supper. Finally, Vasquez abandoned the idea. Certainly he himself could not gallop into San Jose unnoticed.

Vasquez soon had his men at work, however, riding in groups of two or three to hold up travelers along the roads to get themselves prepared for bigger things. Although it was not yet clear to the public that Vasquez was active once more, Sheriffs Rowland and Adams were aware of it quickly enough. They had no trouble perceiving that the robberies were the handiwork of Tiburcio Vasquez. Adams heard from someone that the bandit was once again hiding in the vicinity of New Idria and he went immediately to Salinas to enlist the help of Monterey County Sheriff Tom Wasson. The two of them, along with a few men and a *San Francisco Chronicle* reporter, spent a week or so hunting for Vasquez all around the Panoche Mountains, but never found him. As usual, *Mexicanos* living in the region were willing to shelter him and his men and to offer blank looks when questioned by the frustrated *gringo* lawmen, who felt they were dealing with "stupid greasers." One small episode was particularly upsetting to the *yanquis* and caused the level of heat to rise around the gang. This began when Chavez rode over into the nearby Cholame Valley, where he met Anastacio Androtio, referred to by writer Eugene Sawyer as "a desperado." The two of them came across a sheep herder who happened to have about $200 in preparation for a trip east, so of course they killed him and took the money. Chavez and Androtio were unaware that two men concealed nearby saw them shoot the sheep man three times, then cut his throat from ear to ear. The witnesses were especially horrified to see Chavez cut a cross on the dead man's forehead and pull the skin down over his mouth.

After the man's pockets were emptied and his body was thrown into a ravine, Chavez gave Androtio a $20 gold note and $7.50 in coin, keeping the rest. Chavez apparently had learned from Vasquez that the captain in any operation deserved the lion's share. As soon as this was done, Chavez mounted his sorrel and galloped off. The other horse became frightened, somehow, and ran away, leaving Androtio to walk. The hidden witnesses were able to tell other men in the vicinity. Androtio was taken into custody, confessed and was hanged.

The word was soon out that Chavez, known to be the lieutenant of Tiburcio Vasquez, had perpetrated a particularly vicious crime.

At this point, Vasquez decided to make a grand strike, assembling enough men to attack an entire town and enlarging the fame that had come with the Tres Pinos attack. He chose Kingston south of Fresno because it was a flourishing place on the bank of the Kings River and afforded a quick escape back up into the hills. It was across the river from the town of Laton and had been called Whitmore's Ferry, then Kings River Station before being named simply Kingston. It is not to be confused with the present-day city of Kingsburg, a few miles to the northeast. A small hotel and two stores stood close together on the single street, all near the toll bridge that spanned the river. There was also a stable operated by an *Americano* named O.H. Bliss, who owned the bridge. Kingston appeared to be a perfect target for Vasquez to open his new campaign.

So, on the night after Christmas, 1873--five months after the raid on Snyder's store at Tres Pinos--Vasquez gathered a party of eight men about five miles north of the town on the far side of the river. The bandits had arrived there separately, by different routes, so as not to attract any attention. They waited until darkness and rode to the edge of the river, where they hid their horses in a thicket. Then they walked across the bridge, fanned out through the street and began making their presence known with drawn pistols and Henry rifles. Chavez and another of the raiders came across Bliss himself walking out of the stable and ordered him to lie down. They tied his hands and legs together, then went through his pockets. He had only nine dollars. As George Beers noted in his book on Vasquez, one of the bandits placed a horse blanket under Bliss's head so that he would not be so uncomfortable while lying there, bound on the ground.

In the meantime, other bandits had gone into the Jacobs & Epstein store and the S. Sweet store and within several minutes had at least 30 men tied up and relieved of watches, rings and purses while proceeding to empty safes and money drawers. One of the victims, identified by Beers as a P. Bozeman, had $180 on him. The bandits took it.

In the saloon next to Reichart's Hotel there were 10 or 12 men drinking, it being Friday evening and still the holiday season. Vasquez walked in with four of his men and leveled his rifle at them, calling out, "Anyone who doesn't get down on the floor will die!" It took them no more than a moment or two to reflect upon the sight of his rifle and the pistols in the hands of his men. Then glasses hit the bar and the patrons scrambled to see who could be first face-down on the floor. Vasquez saved them the trouble of carrying their watches and jewelry home that night.

Here is a portion of Beers' account:

> From the proprietor of the hotel they took $400 and a watch, and from the guests, various amounts.
>
> Ed Douglas, a plucky gentleman from Visalia, whom Vasquez and Chavez discovered in the sitting room, peremptorily refused to lie down, when Chavez knocked him down with his revolver, and Vasquez took his money and watch. Lance Gilroy, of Fresno, was eating his supper when these initiatory proceedings were transpiring. Blas Bicuna rudely entered the dining room door, and Mrs. Reichart, terrified by the ominous glance of his eye and the cocked revolver in his hand, emitted a piercing scream and fled from the apartment.
>
> Gilroy, startled by the shrill yell, sprang to his feet and, thinking it was some drunken loafer who had insulted the young lady, before Bicuna comprehended his design, the gallant Gilroy had felled the ruffian to the floor with a chair.

Gilroy's "triumph was short-lived," Beers reported. The "heavy thud of Bicuna's carcass on the floor" quickly attracted another of the gang, Gomez, who sprang in through the doorway and "brought the belligerent gentleman to terms by a strong blow over the head with a Dragon pistol."

Meanwhile, the other robbers were having a little difficulty inside Jacobs & Epstein, where they first ordered clerk Ed Ellinger to lie down on the floor, only to have him run out the door and into Sweet's store "with hair erect and eyeballs protruding like those of a French manikin, exclaiming in tones that froze the merchant's blood, 'The robbers have come!' " Sweet thrust his head out the door to see what was going on. He was instantly seized by one of the bandits who threw him down and tied him.

Although clerk Ellinger had departed hurriedly from Jacobs & Epstein, the others present were hastily thrown to the floor and bound. Lewis Epstein was grabbed and the robbers demanded the key to his safe. At first he insisted that Ellinger had taken it with him. Vasquez made his appearance at that moment, however, and told Epstein that if he did not produce it quickly, his brains would be blown out. Epstein handed it over. The safe was opened and cleaned out. An unknown amount was lifted from the pockets of customers and employees.

Sweet's store was the next target. The gang was just getting started there when two citizens named J.W. Sutherland and James E. Flood heard about the robbery and came on the run with weapons. As Beers recorded it, the bandits:

> ...had taken about $60 when the cheerful tones of a Henry rifle interrupted the game. A second shot was heard the next moment and the guard fell heavily against the door, exclaiming in Spanish, "I am shot!"

Vasquez and his men made what Beers called "a precipitate rush for the bridge, firing right and left as they fled." Sutherland tried to head them off, but couldn't. The bandits reached the far side of the river, "vaulted into their saddles" and galloped away as Sutherland and Flood fired after them. One of the shots grazed Gomez in the neck as he rode away. Another bullet struck Cleovardo Chavez in the right leg, inflicting what Beers called "a severe and intensely painful wound."

According to Beers, Vasquez and his men obtained about $2,500 in cash plus a good deal of jewelry in the raid on Kingston. Vasquez was to tell the editor of *The Los Angeles Star* that they got only $800. Perhaps he did not want his own men to learn the total. The $800 reportedly was just the amount he took from the

Jacobs & Epstein safe. Although he was in a jail cell at the time of the interview, it was no doubt in his mind that he would be free again one day and felt it was in his best interests to keep good relations with his regiment.

He had taken watches from Reichart and from Douglas, the man from Visalia who had refused to lie down and whom Chavez had knocked to the floor with a pistol blow to the head. Vasquez promised these gentlemen he would return their timepieces, but in the confusion of escaping when the trouble began, he did not do so. It is doubtful he ever intended to, but it was a nice device to keep them lying there quietly.

About eight miles from Kingston, the bandits stopped at the adobe of a Mexican family, where Chavez' leg wound was taken care of. Gomez, who had received a scratch on the neck, lay low with Chavez for a little while in the tiny town of Posa de Chane. Vasquez kept five men with him and rode on toward Tulare Lake.

They were missing the recruit named Monteres, who had been afraid to cross the bridge with men from the town firing at the fleeing gang. He apparently hid among the trees at the edge of the river, hoping to make his way to the hills on foot when the excitement had cooled down. Sometime after midnight, he did sneak across the bridge, but was captured early the next morning by J.W. Sutherland and two volunteers who had set out to follow the getaway trail.

Monteres claimed not to have known Vasquez or any of his men, but was put on trial and convicted for his part in the robbery. He was sent to prison for 14 years.

The Kingston raid did, indeed, get the attention of the *Americanos*. At least throughout Fresno, Tulare and Kern Counties. Tulare County Sheriff Glascock organized a posse and headed out in an attempt to locate Vasquez and his men. Sheriff Ashmore of Fresno County and Sheriff Coons of Kern County did not launch posses, but sent deputies out around the countryside individually to see what they could learn. The sheriffs of Santa Clara, Monterey and San Joaquin Counties also had posses looking for Vasquez.

While the lawmen were stumbling around, Vasquez went to the Mexican community of Panama on the Kern River where, as he told *The Star*, "myself and party had a carousal of three days, dancing, love-making, et cetera." And, he added, "*El Capitán* Vasquez was quite a favorite with the *señoritas*."

Panama was not far from Bakersfield and it was not long before it was well known where Vasquez was. But by the time the lawmen got themselves organized to come after him, he had left, taking along only Blas Bicuna and riding to Posa de Chane to find out how his lieutenant, Cleovaro Chavez, was doing. He was happy to discover that Chavez had almost fully recovered from the wound he suffered in the escape from Kingston. He was ready to ride again.

For the next several weeks, during the winter of 1873-1874, Vasquez remained relatively quiet, waiting for spring when there would be plenty of grass for the horses. In the meantime, he went with Chavez back to the Soledad Canyon and Elizabeth Lake areas of Southern California, visiting with old friends and planning for the major operations to come.

The Kingston raid had stirred the state government to action. The Legislature had passed a bill appropriating $15,000 to pay for efforts to capture Vasquez and his men. By January, Governor Newton Booth apparently decided that the sheriffs and their posses needed help from the public. He issued a proclamation offering a reward of $3,000 for the arrest of Vasquez if alive. If he was killed, the reward would only be $2,000. It wasn't long before he increased the figures to $8,000 alive and $6,000 dead.

Vasquez may have found some comfort in the governor's apparent anxiety to keep him alive--but not much. Perhaps it was the smell of the money, or perhaps it was only that *yanqui* settlers were feeling apprehensive after the Kingston raid. Whatever the reason, there was a sharp rise in the number of vigilante groups formed from the Los Angeles area north through the San Joaquin Valley.

Vasquez would have enjoyed the subsequent words of reporter Beers:

> The officers of Kern, Los Angeles, Tulare and Fresno were continually on the alert during the winter for some clue that would lead to the arrest of Vasquez or any of his gang, and every man who had to move about much in the sparsely settled portions of that region constituted himself a volunteer detective; and every passing Mexican was closely scrutinized with the eye of suspicion.
>
> There were dozens of vaqueros, hunters and others who claimed to have met him (Vasquez), and a good many who were nearly certain they had met him, but scarcely any two of them agreed in their description of him. And the disposition of many to "draw the long bow" in telling what they knew or supposed they knew about him greatly embarrassed the officers who were seeking information and added to the security of the bandit, who seemed to bear a charmed life, and to be everywhere and nowhere at the same time.
>
> There were hundreds of brave men in Kern and the adjoining counties who would face him and all the Mexican desperadoes he could rake and scrape in the whole country, or would pursue him into the mountain fastnesses and beard him in his den, if the locality of the den could only be found. There was the rub.

Vasquez may have been sufficiently honored by the reward offers that he felt it was time to show the governor he was still alive and dedicated to his work. He and Chavez decided to see how they might do at the Coyote Hole stagecoach station on the

Los Angeles-Owens River stage road. Beers and Greenwood said this event occurred on Feb. 25, 1874. Sawyer insisted that it was on Feb. 26. Author Remi Nadeau referred to it as Coyote *Holes*. All of this makes little difference, except as another example of the failure of *yanqui* historians to agree on anything concerning Vasquez. Coyote Hole was called "Ass Hole" by the men who frequented it--even after a U.S. Geological Survey team insisted on giving it a more acceptable name on a map.

As Vasquez and Chavez rode toward the station, they met an *Americano* nearby and were obliged to tie him to a tree so that he would not ride ahead and warn anyone that they were in the vicinity. As they neared the old wooden house that served as the stage station, they began firing into the roof with their Henry rifles. Vasquez told Chavez to remain a short distance back, from where he could cover the station and the stables. Vasquez rode alone to the front and called to those inside, "Come out, everyone, or I will burn the house!"

A woman appeared half-hidden in the doorway. "Who are you?" she asked in a trembling voice. "What do you want?"

"I am Tiburcio Vasquez," the bandit told her, not unkindly. "Tell everyone to come out. I will not injure them if they obey." What he really wanted was to be waiting in the station when the Wells Fargo stage arrived in a little while.

The woman drew back and in a few moments about 20 men came filing out with their hands up. The woman followed them fearfully. Vasquez swung down out of his saddle and ordered all of them to sit on the ground. There was a Mexican teamster among them. Vasquez instructed him to take off his hat and stand by to assist. Then he called the gringos forward one by one and commanded them to turn out their pockets, putting into the hat their money along with whatever jewelry and watches they happened to have. Vasquez reportedly excused the woman from having to donate, as it did not appear she had anything of value anyway. He kept the rifle cocked to make certain no one tried to put himself in the history books with a foolish attempt to capture Tiburcio Vasquez.

When all had been searched and the *Mexicano* had handed over the hat half filled with *yanqui* banknotes, coins, rings and watches, Vasquez marched the entire company--including the woman--at rifle point up a small hill behind the station and ordered them to sit down out of sight in some tall brush. He called to Chavez, who came riding up the slope from his post and who remained there to guard them. Then Vasquez walked back down to wait for the stage.

As he approached the livery stable behind the house, it occurred to him that he had not inspected it to make certain no one was hiding in it. As it turned out, there was a drunken *gringo* there. His name, according to Beers, was W.P. Shore, a hunter known simply as "Texas." When Vasquez confronted him in the stable, the man staggered out into the sunlight and demanded, "What the hell's up?" Texans were still resentful over what General Santa Anna had done at the Alamo. They were even quicker than other *yanquis* to sneer at the sight of any *Mexicano*. Vasquez ordered him to sit down inside the stable, but Shore was standing in some mud and did not like the idea at all. He drew his revolver and drunkenly fired a shot that came nowhere close to Vasquez. The bandit, however, did not react kindly to being shot at. He raised his rifle, took aim at the man's right thigh and pulled the trigger. "Texas" flopped into the mud, holding his leg and staring at Vasquez in disbelief. "The next time I order, you obey," Vasquez told him.

The man cooperated then to the extent of tossing away his revolver and blearily studying the bloody wound. Vasquez left him there and went back to the station house to await the stage. When it rattled up in front with dust rolling and the horses snorting, he stepped out onto the porch and pointed his rifle at the startled driver. "Stop!" Vasquez commanded. "Hold up your hands!"

The driver raised his whip as though to lash the horses and pull away. But he was dissuaded by a man sitting beside him. This turned out to be Mortimer W. Belshaw, one of the owners of the Cerro Gordo mine. Vasquez tapped the barrel of his rifle and advised the driver, "Tell your passengers to come out."

As Belshaw and the driver clambered down from the top, three other men climbed out of the coach and sat on the ground as ordered. Vasquez told the driver to unhitch his team. While the driver was doing that, Vasquez leaned his rifle against the wooden porch of the stage station and thrust the pistol from his holster into his belt to make it more quickly reachable. Then he had the passengers walk to him one at a time so he could make them turn out their pockets and examine them closely for watches and jewelry.

From one of the men he took a pair of good leather gloves. The passenger asked Vasquez to return them. "How much are they worth?" the bandit asked him.

"One dollar and a half."

"Well," Vasquez replied, "I will pay you for them. I need them." And he handed back two of the dollars he had taken from him.

From another man Vasquez took a small spyglass. Seeing that Vasquez had not reacted violently to the request for the return of the gloves, this one asked that he be allowed to keep his spyglass. "No, no," Vasquez said. "I have looked a long time for such an instrument and have particular use for it." He did not offer to pay. Do that too many times and one is a poor man, was his motto.

All Vasquez got from the passengers was a few hundred dollars. But he was more disappointed in the contents of the green Wells Fargo box, which he forced the driver to open and which contained some law books as well as bank drafts and mining stocks. These were of no use to him. He did not really think a bank would be willing to pay him for them. In his disgust, he hurled several thousand dollars worth of certificates into the wind and watched them blow away, plastering themselves up against a wooden fence or fluttering across a weed-filled slope. He probably enjoyed the expressions on the faces of the *gringos*.

All he got from Belshaw, the supposed silver magnate of Inyo County, was a watch, $20 in gold and a new pair of boots. Belshaw relinquished them without protest and sat staring at a hole in his stocking.

"*Señor* Belshaw," Vasquez warned him, "if I ever catch you on this road again and you haven't got a thousand dollars for me, your travels will be ended."

Belshaw made no reply.

Vasquez and Chavez did not bother to tie up any of the prisoners, including those they had marched up the hill before the stage arrived. Rather, all of them were ordered inside the station. The bandits then rounded up all the horses in the place and took them away. Six of the horses, including the four that had been hitched to the stage, belonged to the stage company. Two other horses in the stable belonged to those who were robbed. There had not been that much money and the pair meant to get something for all their trouble.

They headed back in the direction of Los Angeles.

On the following day, they halted the Los Angeles-Havilah stage between Soledad Canyon and Mill Station, robbing a half dozen passengers of about $300, tying them up and galloping away.

A few hours later, they took a wagon and six horses from Harper's stable near Soledad.

They also stopped a teamster on the road and took a few dollars from him. These raids managed to stir up all of Southern California. The northern and central parts of the state had already been excited. More vigilante groups were being formed. The bandits set up camp in the Soledad Canyon area of Los Angeles County. The black marks of their campfires may still be seen today on the boulders of what has come to be known as Vasquez Rocks. Tiburcio Vasquez may have spent much time at the rocks staring into his campfire and reflecting that so far he had failed to make the strike he needed to raise a real army of revolution. First of all, Henry Miller the cattle baron had been inconsiderate, failing to show up at Firebaugh's Ferry with $30,000 as Vasquez had been led to believe he would. Then the Southern Pacific Railroad had shown its untrustworthiness by running its train through the countryside above Gilroy ahead of schedule--before Vasquez and his men could derail it. Nor had the Kingston and Coyote Hole raids yielded as much as he had hoped for.

Soon, Vasquez knew, he must succeed with a really profitable venture.

Chapter 14
THE INTREPID SHERIFF

I knew every movement Morse made. I have been around his camp night after night, but have never been near enough to Morse to recognize him, and should not know him if I met him on the road.

It must have been a humiliating thing for Sheriff Harry N. Morse of Alameda County that he was not the one to finally capture Tiburcio Vasquez, who seems to have become his life's obsession. Morse had earned a wide reputation as a fearless, smart lawman who could spend many sleepless days and nights in the saddle until he at last found the man he was looking for. His record in this regard was so good, that Governor Newton Booth sent for him in January of 1874 and commissioned him to form a company that would comb the state for Vasquez.

It was to be the crowning achievement of Morse's career. It is ironic--and perhaps amusing to Vasquez--that another *gringo* sheriff doublecrossed Morse out of the honor of the capture.

Vasquez probably first heard of Morse from newly arriving inmates while in San Quentin for his second term. At the time, of course, he had no way of knowing that the sheriff was to shoot his old friend Juan Soto to death soon thereafter or that he would brazenly walk into a San Francisco saloon and capture another of his *compadres*, Tomaso Redundo. Or that he would be selected by the governor to hunt Vasquez down. Vasquez only knew that Morse was becoming famous for his exploits. He may have been interested in knowing all about him, because Vasquez intended to lead his people against the *yanquis* and sensed that he would be a principal adversary.

Morse became almost as big a legend as the semi-fictitious Joaquin. After retiring as sheriff, he was famous in San Francisco as--of all things, considering the era--a private detective. It is difficult to know how much of what was written about him one can believe, any more than one can accept most of the things said about Vasquez. For example, the profile of Harry Morse published by historian Hubert Howe Bancroft claimed that Morse went to sea at the age of 10 and came to California by shipping around the Horn when he was just 14.

Harry Morse was born in New York City on February 22, 1835--just a few months before Tiburcio Vasquez was born in Monterey, on the opposite side of the continent. Morse was, according to his biographers, the descendent of a Puritan who had arrived in New England just 200 years earlier and had founded the town of Dedham, Massachusetts. Harry Morse's father, Abraham Morse, was a tailor. His mother had come as an infant from England. As a boy, it seems, he was very adventurous and his imagination was stirred by the hundreds of bowsprits that lined New York's South Street, which was called the "Street of Ships." There, along the East River, were the tall windjammers and the European packets, as well as the ships that sailed around the Horn to California, trading boots and fine New England clothing for cowhides.

In this respect, the two boyhoods apparently had some similarity. Tiburcio Vasquez was said to have daydreamed as he saw ships--perhaps some of the same ones--that dropped anchor in Monterey Bay and to have wanted nothing more than to sail away on one of them to the South Seas.

It is possible that young Morse had read Richard Henry Dana's *Two Years Before the Mast*, which was published when Morse was only five years old. One would not think that Dana's descriptions of floggings and general mistreatment of sailors making the voyage around the Horn to California would have inspired anyone to go to sea. But Harry Morse was the kind of *yanqui* who probably was attracted by the challenge. In 1845, if the Bancroft profile is to be believed, Harry's parents agreed to let him ship out on a mail packet sailing between New York and Liverpool. It was said that he refused to go as a cabin boy, signing on before the mast as an ordinary seaman. Supposedly, he pursued that career for four years, until 1849.

By then, gold had been discovered in California, which meant a sea of *yanquis* flooding westward, pushing *Mexicanos* off the land and shooting or hanging them when they objected. There was hardly a crewman on any ship who wasn't planning to find a berth around the Horn so he could try his luck in the gold fields. Harry signed on aboard the Panama, an old East India Packet that had been purchased by a group of men for a trip to California. There were no plans to make a return voyage.

Many of the crewmen were masters and mates of other vessels who were so eager to get to California that they were working for their passage. In addition to future Alameda County Sheriff Harry N. Morse, the crew included several ambitious young men who were to become some of San Francisco's most prominent citizens. Others turned out to be the kind of drunks and drifters who amused themselves by hanging *Mexicanos*.

After a 186-day voyage, during which the little packet spent six weeks battling a Cape Horn storm and lost one man over the side, the gaunt and half-dead sailors saw the Golden Gate off the starboard bow. San Francisco bay was crowded with other vessels at anchor. Most of them were deserted. Their crews had gone ashore as soon as possible, abandoning their seagoing berths to try their luck in the Sierra streambeds. And that, of course, was the intent of every man aboard the Panama. As soon as the anchor was down, the captain of the port came aboard and took possession of the ship. In a very short time, there were several small boats around, ready to take the crew ashore for a price.

So Harry N. Morse, with his seabag slung over his shoulder and his canvas cap on the back of his head, soon found himself standing at the foot of Mission Street in San Francisco, not quite certain where he should go, but confident that his future was the color of gold. He had lost track of the date. He knew only that it was early May of 1849. He could not know that in the village of Monterey, a day's ride to the south, a *Californio* boy just about his age was becoming a man in his own way.

San Francisco was already a big town, with maybe a couple of hundred wooden buildings and as many as 800 people. At Yerba Buena Cove, bales of merchandise were strewn around, piled up with boxes and barrels that had been left there by dock workers who had run off to the gold fields.

Morse first needed a job to raise enough money to go to the gold fields himself. He found a rooming house in which to live and, although he had never cooked before, got a job cooking for sailors at $5 a day. He did that for about a month, then went to Angels' Camp in Calaveras County to try his luck mining. Like most of the others who had rushed in from the East with notions of becoming wealthy in a few days, he knew absolutely nothing about mining. The best miners were *Mexicanos* from Sonora or from New Mexico. There were, as might be expected, many fights as the *yanquis* took away what gold the *Mexicanos* found.

Morse had only mediocre success, but managed to save some money, despite the fact that in the camps a hundred pounds of flour cost $30 and potatoes were 40 cents a pound. He moved on to Mormon Gulch in Tuolomne County and then to what later was called Sonora, after the Mexican state from which so many of the miners had come. After nearly 10 months, he could see he was not going to be a rich man scraping the hills and streams like all the others.

He returned to San Francisco, where he invested his savings in several small boats. With these, he ferried passengers from arriving steamers to the foot of Mission Street. He was already a shrewd businessman. He also used his boats to carry coal and ballast sand out to the steamers. That continued until the middle of 1851--shortly before Tiburcio Vasquez and Anastacio Garcia went to the fandango where the *Americano* constable was killed. At that point, according to the Bancroft manuscript, Morse went to work for the Dallam Bros. bakery at the corner of Mission and First Streets. He drove the delivery wagon, taking bread to all the hotels in San Francisco.

Since arriving in California, Morse had grown more than 10 inches. He was now rangy and tough.

In 1852, he left the bakery and went to Redwood City, where he borrowed enough money to build the Eurcka House, the town's first hotel. Morse supposedly drew the plans, did the carpentry, the papering and the painting. There was no end, one gathers, to his talents. He tried running the hotel for a while with another man named D.W. Balch. Both were Whigs and both were active in Redwood City politics. But eventually Morse turned the Eureka House over to Balch, because much of the construction money had come from the latter's brothers, and he returned to San Francisco.

He was now 18.

So was Vasquez, who also was a successful businessman dealing in cattle, horses and an occasional stagecoach.

Morse moved across the bay to Oakland, where he went to work for an uncle in the butcher business. The uncle died and Morse took over. He acquired a partner, who one day went off with the enterprise's money to buy cattle and never returned. D.W. Balch came up from Redwood City (there is no mention in the Bancroft profile of why Balch left Eureka House) and joined

Morse in a butcher business in Trinity County, in the Sierra foothills.

It wasn't long before the two of them were back in Oakland engaging in the same business there. Morse, it seems, drove the first butcher wagon that ever went out of Oakland selling meat. In 1858, when he was 23 years old, according to Charles Howard Shinn in his *Graphic Description of Pacific Coast Outlaws*, Morse had become an express wagon driver and performed his first publicly noted feat of heroism. Shinn quoted a story that ran as a reminiscence in *The San Francisco Call* 20 years after the incident. Just how accurate it was after all that time is open to question. The description of Morse that Shinn drew from the files of the newspaper was a little too good to be true. Morse, said *The Call*, was aboard the San Francisco Bay ferry boat Contra Costa, which made three round trips a day between San Francisco and "the little town of Oakland" when his daring came into play. The writer of the newspaper piece said Morse was on the seat of his horse-drawn wagon near the bow of the ferry "busily engaged in noting down in a memorandum book his various business engagements for the day." His clothing, said the writer,

> ...was that of a laboring man, consisting of a blue flannel overshirt, pants of coarse material, the legs of which were encased in the uppers of a stout pair of "stogy" boots and on his head he wore a rather broad-brimmed black hat which fitted well down over his face, and from under which protruded a profusion of silken dark-brown hair.
>
> The face was entirely devoid of any beard, and was as smooth as that of a girl. A long, thin nose denoted shrewdness in its possessor, and a pair of dark blue eyes, slightly inclined to gray, looked fearlessly into your own when they were turned toward you. The square, finely cut jaw indicated great firmness of

> character. In fact, the face was one which most people would take a second look at when meeting its owner for the first time. He was well known to all on board as a quiet, determined young fellow who was always ready to fight for his friends, and as equally ready to forgive an enemy. And he had many friends, for he had been through many a tough set-to in protecting the helpless weak against the tyrannical strong.

A 12-year-old boy (described by the *Call* writer as "a light-hearted, merry little fellow, with eyes beaming with the mischievous sport of boyhood") was said to be leaning against the rail that was placed across the forward gangway. Apparently he could not restrain his "youthful exhuberance" and fell over the side about halfway between San Francisco and Oakland. Suddenly, the newspaper said, "a cry of horror went up from the throng of passengers. The rail had lifted from its place and the little fellow, who had stood there a moment before full of life and buoyant enjoyment, fell with a piercing shriek backward into the deep waters of the bay."

Although the ferry was halted and a lifeboat was lowered, the boy was obviously drowning. "In the name of God, why don't that boat get here?" one excited passenger was quoted as shouting. "The boy will sink before they reach him!" Here is the rest of the newspaper story verbatim:

> "Clear the way there," said a low, quiet voice. "Clear the way, and I will save the youngster." All looked toward the speaker. It was the expressman. He was stripped of his hat, shirt and boots. A resolute look shown out of his now wide-awake eyes.
>
> All made way for him. Rushing forward through the throng, he seized a small gangplank that was lying on the upper deck, dragged it to the side of the steamer,

> and with a quick, dexterous movement threw it over the side into the water and plunged over head first after it.
>
> Quick as a flash he rose to the surface, grasped one end of the gangplank and struck out toward the boy, pushing the float ahead of him. "Keep up, Jimmy. Keep up a second more and I will be there," exclaimed the swimmer encouragingly.
>
> When within a few feet of the little fellow, the expressman observed the boy was about exhausted and almost ready to sink, and, with renewed effort, he increased his pace, and came up to him just in time to save him.
>
> A wild hurrah of delight went up from the passengers on the steamer as they saw the little fellow clinging to the gangplank, supported by the strong arm of the expressman. The small boat soon came up and took them aboard the steamer, where both received the congratulations of the passengers. The boat was hoisted on deck, and the Contra Costa continued on her way to the Oakland side.

The newspaper concluded that overblown account by observing that the expressman's name was Harry N. Morse, who became "the intrepid sheriff of Alameda County."

Morse started his own grocery business, but apparently did not find it very exciting. In 1861, just after the War Between the States broke out, Morse and others who backed the Union cause organized the Oakland Guard. Perhaps its members expected the war to come to California. It did not. Morse, however, worked his way up to the position of major general.

In 1863, when he was 27, Morse was appointed deputy provost marshal for Alameda County. He sold his grocery business and the next year was elected sheriff. He was to be re-elected to six more terms, so he held the job for 14 years.

Writer Charles Howard Shinn, in his book about what he called "Pacific Coast outlaws," said Morse carefully studied "the low Mexican cut-throat class" long before he became sheriff. Morse claimed to have had an encounter as early as 1854 with Felipe Carabagal, accused by *yanqui* settlers of committing murders and robberies in the foothills east of San Francisco Bay. Carabagal was feared by ranchers from Martinez and San Pablo to Santa Clara and Gilroy. Morse was driving a buggy on a road in what was to become East Oakland when Carabagal and another *Mexicano* rode up behind and tried to lasso him. Morse was unarmed, so he whipped his horse hard and managed to get away.

At the time Morse became sheriff, Shinn wrote, "a great many men of the Mexican desperado type terrorized Alameda and Contra Costa" (Counties). Shinn, apparently, did not share Tiburcio Vasquez' view that these men were simply trying to take back from the *gringos* what the *gringos* had stripped from Californians.

The bandits lived in the ruins of old adobes scattered through the hills east of Sunol Valley, in the Black Hills at the foot of Monte Diablo and in the wooded canyons near Livermore. These areas, Shinn said, were "unsafe for travelers, unless numerous and well armed." No one, he wrote, "dared to disturb the Mexicans who lived there, and it was considered almost certain death for a white man to venture among them." One old house in the Livermore Valley was kept by Oronio Ramirez, Shinn said, and was a notorious hangout for the likes of Joaquin Murrieta, Procopio, Chilean horse thief Noratto Ponce, Juan Soto, Pancho Ruiz, José California "and a score of other wild fellows used to assemble there."

All this, of course, was before Tiburcio Vasquez had become a major figure throughout California.

Yanqui settlers were moving into the area, but their sheep and cattle were driven off regularly. Morse first studied the topography, riding alone through the countryside trying to locate the hideouts of the outlaws. After a year he knew the territory as well as some of the bandits he was hunting, but he bided his time until he understood as much as he could about them, their habits and appearances. He wrote to the sheriffs of other counties and found out everything he could about the more notorious outlaws.

Suddenly, Shinn wrote, Morse "began to reveal the iron hand under the silken glove." He obtained warrants against one leader after another and served them, "in many cases single-handed and alone, going to their camps and fandangos, appearing when they thought him miles away, and living in the saddle with the same freedom and courage that they themselves possessed."

One of the first encounters to bring Morse favorable press notices was that with Narcisco Bojorques, who had come from the southern part of the state and boasted that he would kill the famous Morse on sight. Bojorques was accused of having led several companions on a raid in the Corral Hollow area in 1863 (about the time Morse became a sheriff) and of murdering a *gringo* with his wife and child, then hanging their *vaquero* from a tree before robbing and burning the family's cabin.

Morse eventually heard that Bojorques was at the Mission San Jose and rode there to make the arrest, but Borjorques fled. Morse pursued him, overtaking him in Sunol Valley. Bojorques was waiting and got the drop on Morse, pointing a pistol at him from close range. But the weapon misfired and Morse shot him in the side. Wounded, Bojorques managed to ride into the chaparral and escape. Five months later, he was killed by the American outlaw One-Eyed Jack in a cantina near Copperopolis.

Although Morse was not the one who ended the career of Bojorques, the encounter did much to spread the story that the sheriff had a charmed life.

In his search for Bojorques, before One-Eyed Jack took care of the matter, Morse led a posse up Arroyo Valle in the Livermore area, where he did not find the man he was looking for, but did find what Shinn referred to as "three notorious Mexicans." One of the Mexicans was named Davila, who was known as *El Capitán*. He had escaped from the Monterey County Jail. Morse arrested him, tied him on a horse and took him in. Morse was not one to return to town empty-handed.

The next adventure for Morse was in 1865, when he tangled with Noratto Ponce. The sheriff's interest in the Chilean horse thief began when Ponce shot an old man to death in Hayward, then walked coolly up to the bar, had a drink and asked if anyone else wanted some of the same. When nobody answered, Ponce got on his horse and rode away. Morse quickly learned that Ponce was in the Black Hills south of Livermore. He went to the area and lay in wait for him at night beside a road that led past some haystacks. As Ponce rode toward his position, Morse jumped out with his rifle and ordered Ponce to surrender. Ponce drew his own pistol and fired. Morse shot back. A deputy accompanying Morse also opened fire. The Chilean's horse was struck by one or more of the bullets and fell. Ponce ran off into the darkness. Morse set fire to the haystacks and lit up the area for miles around, but he could not find Ponce.

When daylight came, he found some spatters of blood and a bloody coat that had been discarded. He also found Ponce's hat. Ponce, however, was nowhere to be seen. Morse and his deputy finally gave up the search.

Six weeks later, he heard that Ponce was recovering at the adobe of an old Spaniard. Morse went there with two officers, but Ponce had gone to his regular hideout in Pinole Canyon at the west end of Contra Costa County. Morse and his men went there, searching the adobes of Mexicans until they came to the last one in the gulch. Ponce ran from the house and dashed toward the brush, exchanging shots with the officers. Morse galloped after him on horseback, aiming his rifle and ordering Ponce to surrender. Ponce pointed his revolver at Morse. But the sheriff fired. Ponce fell dead.

Morse's fame grew. Again, a man had pointed a gun at him without killing or even wounding him. Obviously he was protected by the devil.

That protection served him well again during his encounter with Joe Newell, a drunken *gringo* who had murdered an old settler. Morse and a deputy went looking for Newell, riding the hills in wider and wider circles for 41 days. They covered 1,200 miles and crossed the Sierra Nevada twice. They finally found Newell near Fort Tejon in the south, arrested him and took him back for trial.

After Newell was released, he was living in "Little Mexico," an adobe village near Livermore. Morse rode into the town and Newell took a shot at him, but missed. The sheriff chased him into a gambling house, threw him to the floor and beat him severely.

Morse's fame grew even more with his calm capture of Vasquez' old friend, Procopio

There were numerous other stories about Harry Morse, including the one about the time he rode 150 miles to track down Jesús Tejada for the killing a year before of an Italian storekeeper, a clerk, two *Mexicanos* and a black man near Stockton. Morse and his deputies found Tejada's camp and raided it, capturing Tejada and six other men.

His most famous confrontation, of course, was with Vasquez' old friend Juan Soto, which has already been related. In the duel with Soto, Morse was not hit, despite the number of shots fired at him. One of his own bullets even struck Soto's pistol, jamming the cylinder. Finally, he shot Soto in the head, killing him.

The man did have a charmed life. It was no wonder that Governor Booth finally sent for him to track down and arrest Tiburcio Vasquez.

Chapter 15
AN OLD MAN'S MONEY

I wandered around in the mountains after that until the time of the Repetto robbery.

It seemed to Vasquez, as he was suggesting to editor Truman with this statement, that he should not be too active for a time. He was well aware that Harry Morse was pushing his men hard in the search for him. Los Angeles County Sheriff Billy Rowland and the sheriffs of half the other counties in the state also were on the prowl, hoping to beat Morse to Vasquez. The bandit's friends among the *Mexicano* population kept him informed about the movements of the various posses. Vasquez had become a very hot item because of the raids on Kingston and Coyote Hole, not to mention the holdup of the stage near Mills Station and other operations on the Tulare plains. And of course the triple killing at Tres Pinos was still on every *yanqui* mind.

By this time, Rosario had turned up in San Jose and was claiming that Vasquez had abducted her from Jim Heffner's ranch, had abused her, then abandoned her in the hills. When her story was published by *The San Francisco Chronicle*, the picture of Vasquez as a brutal criminal was complete. The terrified *Americanos* of California were ready to believe it.

Once again, Vasquez' fondness for the opposite sex had brought him trouble.

The legislature appropriated $5,000 to finance the Morse expedition. Gov. Newton Booth had given the Alameda County sheriff a free hand in selecting his men. The posse was made up of some of the leading law enforcement officers in the state, including San Joaquin County Sheriff Thomas Cunningham, Deputy Sheriff Harry Thomas of Fresno County, former Santa Cruz County Sheriff Ambrose Calderwood and Ralph Faville, one of Morse's Alameda County deputy sheriffs. Also in the group were A. J. McDonald of Sunol and Ramon Romero of San Leandro, probably selected for their shooting skills. There was no one in the party from the Santa Clara Sheriff's Department, an oversight that apparently was to cause Morse a small problem.

Another member of the Morse posse was none other than A.B. Henderson, news editor of *The Chronicle*, which made him an early version of the present-time civilian "ride-along." It showed that Morse was not afraid of a little publicity. The public soon began to read about his remarkable endurance in the mountains and the elaborate disguises he wore when trying to learn of Vasquez' whereabouts. The sheriff sometimes put on a red beard and wig as well as dark green goggles. It is not known whether the people he questioned in the little Mexican communities were sufficiently fooled by his disguises to take him for nothing but a mildly curious traveler. Perhaps they were laughing at him.

On March 12, 1874, Morse led his expedition south on a two-month search for the phantom of the canyons, Vasquez. The sheriff and his men rode nearly 3,000 miles through some of the roughest country in the state--without success. In the meantime, Governor Booth had issued his proclamation increasing the reward on Vasquez to $8,000 if taken alive and $6,000 if delivered dead.

This, of course, would have confronted anyone managing to catch Tiburcio alive with a dilemma. It would cost $2,000 to kill him. Possibly Vasquez found that comforting.

It is interesting to note that after Vasquez was captured by Sheriff Rowland in Los Angeles County, thereby cheating Morse of the glory, the latter sought at least some of the credit, writing an almost plaintive letter to the governor:

Oakland, May 30, 1874

Hon. Newton Booth
Sir:

Herewith please find statement of account between the State of California and myself, which if you find correct, you will please forward the balance due me. I disposed of all the things that were left, and salable to the highest bidder. The matting was worn out and not salable, as were the picket ropes. Some of the pickets were lost, also the hatchet, of which I have made no accounting. It was impossible at times to obtain vouchers, being in the mountains, away from pen, ink and paper, and most of the time dealing with the natives who could neither read or write. It is not necessary for me to go into a detailed account of our hunt, as Vasquez is now in custody. Sufficient is it for me to say that we did 61 days hard work in the saddle, part of the time in the night, through the darkness, and part of the time through heavy rains, never resting but always on the go. We rode 2,720 miles, searching the southern part of the state from the San Joaquin river to the sea coast, and although we did not succeed in getting our man, yet we did the state a good service in this. We broke up many dens of reputed murderers and thieves in places where officers had never ventured to go before.

Sheriff Morse offered no details. How did he mean "broke up"? Were men killed? Were they arrested? Or did they simply vanish into the canyons when they saw the posse coming? As for the term "reputed murderers and thieves," one wonders whether that means particular crimes had been attributed to them, or whether they were simply *Mexicanos* who did not stand at attention when the Morse troops rode past.

Now we get to a little whining in Morse's letter to the governor:

> I regret one thing very much. It is this, that officers in the upper part of the state, to wit, Santa Clara, should have a feeling of jealousy toward myself and party, and make known my whereabouts and plans through the public prints, and thereby making it more difficult for us to do our work properly.

It is not clear what this complaint was all about, but it must be assumed that Sheriff Adams of Santa Clara County and Morse by now were not the best of friends. As we have seen, Morse did not choose Adams to ride with him in the search for Vasquez. Next in the letter to Booth, Morse may well have been biting the inside of his mouth to pretend that he was not furious with Billy Rowland for making the arrest.

> Too much praise cannot be bestowed upon Sheriff Rowland and party for the very able manner in which they carried out their plans, and effected the capture of Vasquez.

But Morse wanted the governor to understand that it could not have been done without him:

> One thing I think is quite certain and that is this. We deserve credit for the thoroughness of our search. Had we not been out, Vasquez would still have been at liberty. At least Vasquez told me so himself. He told me the only thing that kept him about Los Angeles was the fear of meeting my party, he thinking that I was still in the southern part of the state.

Vasquez probably did tell him that. Morse was an interesting man and Vasquez apparently had a great deal of respect for him. With his ability to stay in the saddle for long periods and his knowledge of the mountains and canyons, the sheriff could have been a very good *bandido*--if he had not been devoted to the law.

Of course Morse explained to the governor what a difficult job he had been given:

> It is a good deal like hunting a needle in a hay stack, this hunting a man in the mountains. The only way is to do as was done in the present case, to wit, purchase the information that will lead you to the whereabouts of the party sought, the rest is easy.

To show how all the accounts about Vasquez conflicted, Eugene Sawyer wrote that it was during this period that false rumors indicated Vasquez had sailed for Mexico on the steamer Constitution. Supposedly, a used clothing dealer in San Francisco said that Vasquez had come into his shop and purchased some women's clothing in order to disguise himself and board the ship at San Francisco. A few weeks later, wrote Sawyer, a Mexican arrived in California from Guaymas to say he had seen Vasquez in that Mexican coastal town. As nothing had been seen or heard of Vasquez and his men for a time, Sawyer wrote, "many persons believed that the bandit had really given the officers the slip." But, Sawyer added, "Sheriff Adams of Santa Clara County and Sheriff

Morse of Alameda County were better posted. They had sent out spies and knew that the outlaw was still in California."

Although Vasquez seemingly had made a brief visit to Mexico at the behest of his brothers, who wanted him to remain there, he apparently was not--as Sawyer suggested--out of California during the period that Morse's expedition was looking for him. (As previously noted, writer Dominga Hoffer had Vasquez dressing as a woman and sailing for Mexico three years earlier. Whether Vasquez ever really dressed in the clothes of a woman is not known.)

Morse, to his obvious shame, did not find Vasquez and his gang, who were generally lying low during the two months the Alameda County sheriff and his expedition were riding across the state at the behest of Governor Booth. Despite the rumor that he had slipped off to Mexico, or the belief by some that he had returned to his old haunts in La Cantua Canyon near the New Idria mines, Vasquez seems never to have been far from Los Angeles during this period. He and his men hid out in several places: the hills around Newhall, at Castle Rock near Chatsworth and in Dunsmere Canyon. They spent much of their time at what was to be known as Vasquez Rocks, which has already been mentioned. This is just north of the present-day Antelope Canyon Freeway in the Los Angeles County region of Agua Dulce.

Vasquez also hid out now and then at the adobe of George Allen, known as Greek George, close to what is now Hollywood Boulevard and the mouth of Laurel Canyon. For a price, the Greek could always provide a fine meal cooked by the dark-eyed *señorita* who lived with him.

While Vasquez and his gang remained relatively inactive, he was in all likelihood aware of Morse's efforts as well as those of Billy Rowland, the Los Angeles County sheriff who was not inclined to cooperate with his colleague from the north. After leading a posse or two in search of Vasquez, Rowland seemed content to wait the bandit out. He knew Vasquez was in the area. For one thing, he heard that Vasquez rode into Los Angeles occasionally to visit one or two young women and perhaps play some cards in the Sonora section. But he never caught him at it.

Finally, Vasquez could lie quiet no longer. He needed money. He sent out a young recruit, Lebrado Corona, to scout the area and learn what ranches in the area might be profitable targets. In a few days Corona returned to the rocky ravine to tell Vasquez he had found out that an Italian rancher named Alessandro Repetto had recently sold a large consignment of wool for a great deal of money. The ranch was in the El Monte area, not far from the San Gabriel Mission.

Vasquez, Chavez and Corona rode out to the area of Repetto's ranch, passing themselves off as innocent sheepshearers. Of all the ranch jobs Vasquez might have chosen, sheepshearing was not one of them. A *vaquero* at least was on horseback most of the time and had some variety to his work. The bandit chieftan left his two men camped nearby and approached a sheepherder on the Repetto ranch to ask whether he had seen a brown mustang that had got away. The man said he hadn't. Vasquez spent a little while talking to him and casually looking around to get a good idea of the layout. Then he asked whether *Señor* Repetto was home. The sheepherder shrugged. It was obvious he did not know or really care. Vasquez told him he had to ride to the mission on business, but that if the man could find the missing horse and catch him, there would be $10 in it for him. Maybe even $15. It was a very good horse, Vasquez said.

Vasquez later told Ben Truman in the jail interview that he then returned by a roundabout way to the other two men in the Arroyo Seco. As soon as it was dark, he said, they rode to a spot near Repetto's house and camped for the night. The next morning they went toward the house, where Vasquez left his *compadres* out of sight behind a fence while he approached the sheepherder to ask whether Repetto wanted any herders or shearers. Informed that Repetto was home, Vasquez went to the house "to see if I could bring the *patrón* to terms without killing him."

Vasquez said he told Repetto he was an expert sheepshearer, as were the two men waiting out by the fence. The sheep rancher invited all three inside, where they surrounded him while Vasquez demanded all the money in the house. "At this he commenced hollering," Vasquez told Truman.

After Repetto produced only $80, Vasquez and his men tied both the rancher and his young nephew to a tree. Vasquez demanded money to let them go and told Repetto he was aware of the recent $10,000 sheep sale. The rancher swore he had bought land with most of the money and was untied so he could produce the proof. He brought out a small ledger and bank account book, then began to read the figures to the bandit. But Vasquez interrupted him angrily, insisting that he was able to read. Repetto gave him the books, which Vasquez studied, seeing that there had indeed been a recent deposit of $10,000, but a more recent withdrawal of $9,500. The canvas-bound ledger showed the latter amount had been paid to someone named Roberto Cambriano.

Vasquez subsequently told editor Truman, "I then expressed my regrets for the trouble I had put him to, and offered to compromise. I told him I was in need of money, and that if he would accommodate me with a small sum I would repay him in 30 days with interest at 1½ %."

Repetto protested that he did not have much left in the bank, but would write a check for the $800. That must have amused Vasquez, who could hardly have imagined himself walking into the bank to cash it. He proposed that Repetto's 15-year-old nephew ride into Los Angeles with the check, made out to cash, and bring back the money. He cautioned the youth not to say a word to anyone at the risk of having the old man killed.

While they waited for the nephew to return, Vasquez began cooking breakfast for his two men. He was, after all, a very good cook and Repetto had a well-stocked larder.

When the boy arrived at the Temple and Workman bank in Los Angeles, he was so nervous he was not believed for a moment.

He attempted to present the check, only to be questioned by the bank's suspicious president, P.F. Temple. The boy broke into tears and blurted out the full story of how the three bandits arrived at the ranch demanding money. Temple quickly sent a runner to notify Sheriff Rowland, who had been waiting for just such a break. The sheriff went to the bank and interviewed the frightened boy, then organized a posse in just about a half an hour.

Rowland was no doubt very excited by the prospect of closing in on Tiburcio Vasquez, for whom every sheriff in the state was looking. There was, after all, the reward money. Not to mention the honor of being able to capture Vasquez before Morse could do it.

Rowland's plan was to split his men into three groups--one riding toward the ranch from El Monte, one from Los Angeles and the other at the Los Angeles River to block an escape. Rowland himself rode at the head of seven men. His contingent headed out Aliso Street in a cloud of dust, headed for the Italian's ranch.

At the bank, the boy was in tears. He pleaded for the money, saying his uncle was going to be killed if he did not return to the ranch with it. Temple finally gave him a bag containing only $500 in gold and the boy rode off. He took trails in the hills beyond the river that the sheriff and his men did not know. He reached the ranch ahead of them.

Vasquez seized the bag and was in the process of opening it to make certain he had not been cheated when one of his men, who was posted at the window as a sentry, spotted the riders. Vasquez ran to look out. Just topping the rise two or three miles away were a half dozen mounted men with rifles. "*Vamanos!*" Vasquez yelled. He held onto the bag of gold and the three crashed out the door to their horses, spurring them toward the trees.

It was not difficult to lose the posse. For one thing, the posse's horses were tired from being run at a gallop all the way from the pueblo of Los Angeles. For another, Neither Rowland nor his men knew the ravines and brushy canyons the way Vasquez did. In a very short time, the bandits were in the Arroyo Seco, pushing their horses toward Pasadena.

Once again, Vasquez was able to elude capture.

Chapter 16
THE CAPTURE

I was not expecting company at the time the arrest was made, or the result might have been different.

Presumably, Vasquez was telling interviewer Truman that, had he seen the lawmen approaching Greek George's, there would have been some dead *gringos*.

The fact that a posse was hotly pursuing them as they galloped away from Repetto's sheep ranch did not dampen the gang's enthusiasm for their chosen profession. Certainly not when they saw a wagon carrying three Los Angeles Water Company employees on their way to do some work in the Alhambra area. Vasquez and his two companions had sufficiently outdistanced the sheriff's posse that they felt they could take time out to see what these *yanquis* had to offer. Vasquez ordered them to stop their wagon and hand over their cash. One of the three, Charles E. Miles, a well-known engineer in the area, thought it was a joke. He laughed and was about to get his team moving again. He changed his mind, however, when Vasquez drew his Henry rifle from its scabbard behind his saddle and pointed it at him.

The bandits did not get a great deal of money in that transaction, but did relieve Miles of a gold watch which he seemed disheartened to lose. Vasquez was not to keep it for long, however.

The bandit chief had miscalculated to some degree, because Rowland had not yet given up. His party was in close pursuit. Vasquez, Chavez and Lebrado Corona were concluding their business with Charley Miles and his friends when the dust from the posse blossomed a couple of miles away. Vasquez wished the *Americanos* in the wagon *buenos dias* and the fugitives whipped their horses into a gallop once again, giving the lawmen the slip in the Arroyo Seco. Vasquez and his men probably could have lain in wait for the sheriff and ambushed him, killing all in his party. Chavez reportedly urged him to do this, but Vasquez decided against it, knowing that if they did that, every man in the southern part of the state who could carry a gun would be out looking for them by sunset. Vasquez knew what the effect of such a massacre would be on the non-*Mexicano* population. There might even be American Army troopers brought in from other states to find him.

For a time, however, he may have wished he had followed Chavez' advice. The bandits were not as familiar with that particular area as they might have been. They soon found themselves at the end of a trail, confronted by a steep and almost impassable canyon that was heavily overgrown by manzanita and chaparral. Sheriff Rowland's posse was still in pursuit and there was no chance of doubling back without running into them muzzle to muzzle. The trio managed to get through the thicket and reach the bottom of the canyon, but had to abandon their spent horses in the treacherous terrain. That meant losing saddles and bedrolls, for they could not possibly carry them on foot through the undergrowth.

It also meant leaving the beautiful palomino, which had become almost as famous throughout California as Vasquez himself. Then he began pushing on foot through the brush with Chavez and Corona.

It is not clear whether the lawmen found the horses, but they gave up the chase when darkness closed in on them. They rode back to Los Angeles.

Vasquez and his men hiked for several days, being careful when they camped at night to keep their fires low and hidden in the shelter of large boulders so they could not be seen from far away. Eventually, they reached the mouth of Big Tujunga Canyon, walking down into the valley and into a small *Mexicano* community. They approached the first adobe, where Vasquez greeted the *campesino*, identifying himself and his men. The *Mexicanos* in the settlement were delighted to show hospitality to the famous Tiburcio Vasquez. The bandits were fed and were given beds while the women washed and patched their torn *pantalones* and shirts.

When they were rested and had managed to acquire fresh horses without disturbing the ranchero who felt he owned them, Vasquez, Chavez and Corona said *adiós* to their hosts and left. At this point, Vasquez thought it best that they separate, so Chavez rode off to a *Mexicano* ranch in Soledad Canyon while Vasquez took young Lebrado Corona with him in the direction of Greek George's, a couple of miles beyond Cahuenga Pass near what finally came to be called Nichols Canyon.

At the time Vasquez had been doing business with Alessandro Repetto at his ranch, it seems, the ambitious Alameda County Sheriff Harry N. Morse--still trying to make good on his promise to the governor--was searching for the bandit in the Tehachapi Mountains north of Los Angeles. Wherever Morse went with his troop of deputies and volunteers, he would interview *campesinos* in an effort to learn Vasquez' whereabouts. As most *Mexicanos* in California were anxious to protect Vasquez, Morse collected a great deal of worthless information. People who claimed to know Tiburcio well and to have seen him within the past few days would tell the sheriff that he had gone to Mexico, or back to the northern part of the state, or perhaps to Arizona. Or that he had been killed in a gunfight over yet another man's wife and was buried in an unmarked desert grave. Others offered him blank stares and pretended not to understand his *gringo* Spanish.

At Fort Tejon, however, Morse found someone willing to sell Vasquez out. The man told the determined sheriff he had heard Vasquez was at Greek George's adobe. It was not recorded who the informant was, but Vasquez suspected it was someone from the little *Mexicano* community where he had rested with Chavez and Corona after hiking down out of the Big Tujunga. Greenwood wrote that it apparently was a Mexican guide Vasquez had hired before the Repetto robbery to show him the Arroyo Seco escape route. Vasquez, of course, had help from many local *Mexicanos*, but one suspects he never had to hire one of them. Whoever the man was, it was a good thing for him that Vasquez never knew his name or where to find him, as someone would surely have been dispatched to see that he never talked to another sheriff.

At any rate, Morse apparently felt the information was accurate, for he left his men at Tejon and caught a stage to Los Angeles. There, he met with Sheriff Billy Rowland and suggested that the two of them team their forces to capture Vasquez at Greek George's. Morse was to learn, to his regret, that there is not always honor among lawmen.

Rowland, clearly, had no interest in sharing the trophy with Harry Morse, who in his view already had attracted too much publicity. He told his fellow sheriff from the north that he knew the informant and considered him a cheat and a liar; that there was no use wasting any time following his leads. Joseph Henry Jackson wrote in *Bad Company* that Rowland "appeared to be irritated by Morse's presence in Los Angeles County and gave him to understand that he, Rowland, was competent to handle affairs thereabouts, that he had certain knowledge that Vasquez was not south of the Tehachapi at all but was holed up in the hills whence Morse had just come, and finally that he would be happy if Sheriff Morse would take himself and his men out of Los Angeles County northward again into those same hills where there might be some likelihood of finding the man they were after."

Morse apparently either believed Rowland or felt he had no choice, for he returned by the next stage to Fort Tejon, where he collected his men and rode north. His expedition had failed. He had not found Tiburcio Vasquez. Greenwood noted:

> Had Morse acted independently...he would have captured Vasquez... Interestingly enough, a few weeks after Vasquez was captured, a warrant was drawn by the state treasurer in favor of Rowland for the sum of $8,000.

Harry N. Morse had been double-crossed out of both the reward and the glory.

Hardly had Morse departed for the north than Rowland laid plans to arrest Vasquez at Greek George's place. He apparently meant to lead the raid in order to become famous as the captor of Tiburcio Vasquez, but was persuaded that if he rode out of Los Angeles in the company of armed men, the word would be flashed and Vasquez would slip away once again.

So, on the evening of May 13, 1874, Rowland organized an eight-man posse headed by Undersheriff Albert S. Johnson. It included Los Angeles Chief of Police B.F. Hartley, Major H.M. Mitchell (an attorney and special deputy), Constable J. Sam Bryant, a Los Angeles police detective named Emil Harris, citizen D.K. Smith (who apparently had something to do with confirming for Rowland the information from the man who sold Vasquez out) and W.E. Rogers of the Palace Saloon.

Also going along was George A. Beers, the *San Francisco Chronicle* reporter who subsequently published his highly imaginative biography of Vasquez. Like Morse, Rowland was not against ensuring that there would be adequate public notice of the event.

For a description of this ride, we must rely on the accounts of Greenwood, Ben Truman's *Star* and *The Los Angeles Herald* of May 16, 1874. It is hardly surprising at this point to learn that these sources disagree on numerous points, including the spelling of names. Was it *Johnson* or *Johnston*, for instance? We probably can accept the word of the *Star* and the *Herald* that it was Johnson--only because the reporters were working in the town at that time and not depending on hand-me-down stories decades later.

To avoid attracting attention, the posse members went one by one in the darkness to a corral at 7th and Spring Streets. They saddled up and rode out of the pueblo at 1:30 A.M., heavily armed with pistols and Henry rifles. They proceeded westward across what was to become Hollywood until they reached a bee ranch kept by Major Mitchell, one of their party. This was up a small canyon. It being about 4 A.M. by now, the posse sat down to have some breakfast (no doubt with all the honey they could eat) and to discuss how they were going to get close to Greek George's place. The house was an old L-shaped adobe. At one end of the building was a room used by Vasquez as a lookout spot. From its window he could see for miles to the east (toward Los Angeles), and for a good distance west, making surprise attack difficult.

It was decided that Undersheriff Johnson, Bryant and Mitchell should go ahead and scout the situation. They followed a mountain road to a point about a mile from Greek George's adobe. There was a thick fog, so they settled down and waited for daylight, trying to watch the house as well as they were able.

It was noon before the fog lifted enough so that they could see much. At that time, Major Mitchell trained his field glasses on the adobe and saw a man riding away on a white horse. He thought it might be Vasquez. Mitchell and Johnson discussed whether to follow the horseman while the other members of the posse surrounded the house.

According to Beers, Major Mitchell and D.K. Smith rode off to check out the man on the horse and thus were not in on the actual capture. As this does not jibe too well with other accounts, it is possible that reporter Beers was wrong--even though he was there. In any event, it was Greek George himself who rode away at that time, supposedly having argued with his woman over the attention she was paying to Vasquez and stomping out in a fit of anger, but unwilling to challenge the bandit directly because he chose to remain alive a little while longer.

Before Johnson and Mitchell could decide whether to follow the rider, two *Mexicanos* entered the canyon in a horse-drawn wagon. Hartley stopped them and demanded to know where they were going. They explained that they were headed up into the canyon to get a load of firewood. Johnson and Mitchell decided they had hit upon a method of approaching the house without being seen. The posse members climbed into the back of the wagon and lay flat. Johnson told the driver that if either he or his companion tried to warn Vasquez, he would be shot.

The frightened *Mexicanos* promised they would not.

Beers wrote that Vasquez saw the wagon approaching, but thought nothing of it. He had seen it almost every day that he had been there. He was familiar with the two men and had spoken with them upon occasion when they stopped by the *adobe* on their way to or from their woodcutting. Vasquez and Corona were were just sitting down to a breakfast prepared by the Greek's woman. Vasquez had just taken off his revolvers and had set his rifle down. He was not very interested in the wagon outside, because with George gone for a while, he probably was looking forward to a delicious hour or two with the woman out beneath the trees.

Suddenly she screamed. A plate of food shattered as she dropped it on the floor. Vasquez jumped up from the table and stared out the window. He saw eight armed *Americanos* spilling out of the wagon and running to positions behind trees and rocks around the house. "Bar the door!" he shouted at Corona. It was standing ajar. The woman was faster than Corona. She leaped to the door and slammed it shut, sliding the wooden bar across. Vasquez was scrambling for his revolver, which was hanging in its holster from the back of a chair.

Newspaperman Beers cast himself in a hero's role. Some of what he said probably was true, however. According to Greenwood, Beers and Bryant were the first two to get close to the house. But while the other members of the posse charged forward, Beers saw Vasquez' horse picketed in a clearing and stationed himself and his Henry rifle near the path with a clear view of the window, reasoning that the bandit would come diving out of it to mount and flee. He was correct. As the posse smashed its way into the front of the house, Vasquez hurtled through the small window and sprinted toward his horse. As Beers wrote about it:

> I stepped into the path leading along the west side of the house, and the next instant the agile form of Vasquez came flying toward me, and I fired. He threw up his hands, at the same instant crying out, "No shoot! No shoot!" and Hartley gave him a charge of buckshot from his double-barrel gun.

Whether or not Vasquez cried out any such thing, he apparently stopped, because the rifle shot struck him in the shoulder and spun him around. Then the shotgun went off, and several pellets wounded Vasquez. Undersheriff Johnson and the other posse members closed in on the bandit immediately. Vasquez thought for the moment that he was mortally wounded, but did not give his captors the satisfaction of seeing him go to the ground. He held out his revolver and dropped it. "You have me," he said. "It is over."

Writer Remi Nadeau claimed that Vasquez said, "You boys have got me. My name is Alejandro Martinez."

And that Undersheriff Johnson replied, "I have had your photograph for years and know you to be Tiburcio Vasquez."

Perhaps, but given Vasquez' ego, it seems doubtful he would claim to be someone else.

Another questionable report was that Vasquez complimented the posse members on their bravery. The *Herald* story, which was heavily influenced by the self-serving accounts of the participants, read in part:

> The rest of the inmates of the house were taken without any violence, while some of the party took possession of the house and its occupants, others addressed themselves to caring for the wounded robber. At first it was thought that he was mortally wounded, and this was his own belief, as he expressed it to his captors. Examination, however, showed the wounds not to be so serious as supposed. At the first moment when he gave himself up, Vasquez turned to Hartley and said, "What's your name?" A remark so singular prompted the inquiry subsequently as to his motive in asking the question, when he said, "I wanted to know the name of a brave man. I am not a coward myself, and I like to know another brave man."

In Nadeau's version:

> "You are good men, good men," he complimented his captors. "You have done well."
>
> Embarrassed, one of them ventured, "We are sorry to have had to wound you so."
>
> "It is not your fault," returned Vasquez. "I have been a damned fool. I should not have attempted to escape."

The *Herald* article noted that the posse also took into custody Vasquez' palomino horse, which it referred to as "the famous white horse of Vasquez." As he had been forced to abandon his mount in a canyon and as palominos are not white, this seems unlikely. The story said the officers confiscated three Henry rifles, five six-shooters, 400 rounds of ammunition, a "villainous-looking dirk knife belonging to Vasquez" and some other weapons. Three saddles were also taken, the newspaper reported, "two of them very fine ones, worth probably $50 apiece." The gold watch and chain Vasquez had taken from Miles, the water company engineer he robbed after leaving Repetto's ranch, was also recovered. As the newspaper related, "Vasquez said that if he had known Miles was a working man he would not have asked it of him."

It was over. Two decades of terrorizing settlements, stage coach passengers and lone riders, all in the name of trying to gain sufficient funds to lead his people against the *gringos*. The dreaded Tiburcio Vasquez was finally taken by eight men hiding in a wood wagon.

As one jailhouse interviewer quoted him:

"I regret being taken in this way, for I always expected to sell my life dearly. Now, I suppose, I will be hung like a dog."

Chapter 17
STAR PRISONER

Of Sheriff Rowland and the gentlemen who captured me, I will say they are all brave men. They took desperate chances, and it was one chance in a million that they succeeded. They could have killed me, but did not, and they have treated me in the kindest manner.

No doubt Vasquez thought it wise to be gracious after his capture. The above he said to the *Los Angeles Herald* reporter who was in the bandit's cell questioning him even before Major Truman of *The Star*. At the time, no doubt, Vasquez was doing and saying whatever he felt would make things easier for him in his trial.

San Francisco Chronicle reporter Beers, who had been allowed to go on the raid by the publicity-wise Sheriff Rowland, claimed to be the one who bandaged Vasquez and wrote that the latter told him, "You dress my wounds and nurse me careful, you boys get $8,000! If you let me die, you only get six. You get $2,000 for being kind." This was in reference to the conditional reward offered by the governor. Indeed, Vasquez may well have reminded Beers of the profit to be had in keeping him alive.

Once Vasquez had been wounded and taken into custody, Undersheriff Johnson procured a spring wagon and two mules from a nearby barn. A mattress from inside Greek George's adobe was placed in the wagon and Vasquez was allowed to lie down for the ride into Los Angeles. Now that the hunt was over, he was being treated like a celebrity. Corona was placed in the wagon with him.

Despite the mattress, the trip was not a comfortable one for Vasquez. He was wounded in numerous places and the pain was beginning to set in. He did his best not to let his captors see this, but he was bleeding heavily all over the mattress. As they entered the town, it was clear that the word had spread. One of the party, probably, had ridden ahead to broadcast it. As Beers reported:

> The whole city was thrown into a state of excitement, and by the time we arrived in front of the jail, a crowd of several hundred had assembled, which was constantly increased by fresh arrivals; but, to the credit of the Los Angeles people, not the slightest manifestation of a disposition was made to enforce the lynch law, or in any way to interfere with the due course of the law.

There were even some in the crowd who reportedly applauded and called out, "Hey, Tiburcio!"

As he was eased off the back of the wagon in his blood-soaked clothes and carried by four men up the wooden steps into the stuccoed adobe jailhouse, Vasquez could see several *Mexicanos* gathered quietly on the far side of the street. They were careful not to get in the way of the celebrating *gringos*. They simply watched, unable to believe, probably, that the fabled Vasquez had been captured at last. It would have been in the bandit's nature to smile at them and try to reassure them that it was not yet over for Tiburcio Vasquez.

But it was.

Star Prisoner

Writer Remi Nadeau said in the book *City-Makers* that by the time Sheriff Billy Rowland arrived at the jail, "someone had brought a bottle of whiskey to the outlaw's cell; the rascal had cheerfully accepted a drink and, showing himself equal to the occasion, offered an unexpected toast: 'The President of the United States...' "

Vasquez was put in one cell and Corona was put in the other. The sheriff, aware that Vasquez was worth more alive than dead, wasted no time bringing in a physician to tend to him. Several writers referred to the medical man as "Dr. Wise," but Nadeau identified him as County Physician Joseph P. Widney, the brother of Judge Robert M. Widney, who built Los Angeles' first streetcar line.

Vasquez was laid out on the floor and given whiskey to dull the pain while the shotgun pellets were extracted with knife and tweezers. Buckshot was removed from his left arm, his left leg and from the side of his head. Another pellet, the doctor said, had struck him in the pectoral region, but had passed through. Vasquez may have been almost blind with agony when the doctor applied some of the whiskey to the open wounds, but he refused to flinch. Rather, he laughed and talked while the surgeon probed. None of the pellets had buried themselves deeply enough to require a lengthy operation. Another man, who may or may not have been a doctor also, then dressed Vasquez' wounds with fresh, clean bandages. Vasquez appeared to be so tough, according to Nadeau, that Dr. Widney warned Sheriff Rowland the outlaw "would still be game for a long day's ride."

One of those allowed into the cell to identify Vasquez while the doctor tended to him was Charles E. Miles, the engineer whose gold watch the bandit had taken while riding away from the Repetto ranch robbery. Chief of Police Hartley had already returned the watch to him, having taken it from Vasquez' bloody, punctured coat. But Miles was not satisfied. He complained that the gold chain was missing and asked Vasquez where it was. Vasquez told the doctor, who had not yet left, to look for it in an inside pocket that Rowland's men had overlooked. The chain was returned to Miles, who thanked the bandit.

Another brought by Sheriff Rowland to identify Vasquez as a perpetrator of evil deeds was Alejandro Repetto. The sheep rancher was red-faced and was sweating heavily as he was led into the cell where Vasquez lay, still in blood-caked clothes. With Repetto, too, Vasquez sought to make amends in the hope that it would help him at the trial. "I told you I would repay the money I borrowed from you," the bandit said. "And Vasquez always keeps his word."

Repetto smiled nervously, standing as far from the prisoner as the cramped confines of the cell would permit--as though he expected Vasquez to leap up and seize him by the throat at any moment. "As far as I am concerned, *Señor*, you can settle that little account with God Almighty. I have no hard feelings against you. None whatever. I only ask that, should you ever...resume your affairs, that you not call at my ranch again."

"Ah, *Señor*," Vasquez said, "if I am so unfortunate as to suffer conviction and am compelled to undergo a short term of imprisonment, I will take the earliest opportunity to reimburse you. *Señor* Repetto, I am a gentleman!"

Repetto looked pleadingly at Sheriff Rowland, who opened the cell door and allowed him to depart.

As Vasquez was no longer bleeding, he was placed upon a cot and was left alone. When he finally awoke the next day, he was given a fine suit that Rowland informed him had belonged to a local gambler no longer in need of it. The gambler had been detected hiding an extra ace up his sleeve and had been dispatched by a resentful *vaquero*. Since he had been shot between the eyes, there was no hole in the coat, which Vasquez appreciated. Despite his wounds and the stiffness that had taken over his body, Vasquez was able to put on his new apparel and send his bloody clothes out to be burned. He was also furnished with a good breakfast. The pain was no longer bothering him. He was told that reporters were clamoring to interview him and that others--including some ladies of the town--were anxious to make certain he was comfortable. Before receiving visitors, however, he wished to see what was being said about him. He asked to see the newspaper accounts of his capture and was told by Sheriff Rowland that they were in English; that he would not understand them. Assured by Vasquez that he could read English as well as he could speak it, Rowland provided him with a copy of *The Los Angeles Herald.*

The headlines read:

VASQUEZ CAPTURED

THE ROBBER SEVERELY, BUT NOT FATALLY WOUNDED

A PARTY OF LOS ANGELES MEN REAP THE HONOR OF THE CAPTURE

FULL ACCOUNT OF THE SUCCESS-FUL MANEUVRE WHICH PLACED THE BANDIT IN THE HANDS OF THE LAW

The story began:

> If an earthquake had shaken the foundation of our city and swallowed up one-half of our places scarcely more excitment would have ensued than that which followed the announcement of the capture of Vasquez on Thursday afternoon.
>
> The City Fathers were in profound deliberation in their rooms, when there was a rush outside the door, a

> crowd surged about the place, and somebody said, "Vasquez is caught." The Council adjourned *sine die*, without ceremony.
>
> In front of the entrance to the City Prison there was an extremely warlike display. The Sheriff's party, armed with numberless revolvers, Henry rifles, and shooting irons of various descriptions, had just arrived, convoying a light spring wagon, in which was lying the man long sought for, the veritable Vasquez.

The *Herald* story, after describing the actual capture in some detail--although not with complete accuracy--offered a conclusion that it was a wonder Vasquez was not killed "after standing such a fire as he did, and receiving so many balls." The paper reported that the bandit was very weak from the loss of blood, "but otherwise in as favorable a condition as could be expected."

As for the posse operation that resulted in Vasquez' capture, *The Herald* called it "perfect," noting that although some of the gang remained at large, "still their power is broken, now that their chief is captured. Doubtless the others will soon find the coils tightening about them, so that they will either leave the country or one by one find themselves taken into custody."

It had been a good day for Southern California, declared the newspaper, "a day in which the majesty of the law was vindicated and an effectual check placed upon outlawry in this part of the country forever."

Ben Truman, editor of *The Star*, introduced himself as "Major" immediately upon being ushered into Vasquez' cell by Sheriff Rowland. The latter, incidentally, was in almost constant attendance throughout these interviews, being extremely anxious to have the press know about his cleverness at capturing the famed bandit.

As Truman had been a major in the Army of the United States and still enjoyed being addressed by that title, Vasquez did so. He could not, presumably, help but notice that Truman did not call him *Capitan*, as many of his men did.

Truman reported that the crowd surrounding the jail was well-behaved and that no one tried to interfere with law officers or to lynch Vasquez. He described the general feeling as one "more of relief than of revenge or exultation" and said the citizens seemed to believe that, if convicted, Vasquez would be properly punished. "Woe be, however, to the man who names himself as his successor, and endeavors to emulate his deeds of violence," Truman editorialized. "The people of this part of the state will stand no more brigandage." The editor declared that Chavez and other fugitive members of Vasquez' gang "may well pause before they seek revenge or perpetrate any more robberies."

Truman called the seizure of Vasquez "one of the most interesting chapters in criminal matters that has ever been written." He added:

> The captured robber has defied pursuit, mocked at strategy, and eluded for months the skill of the bravest and most celebrated detectives on the coast. We do not believe that, once afoot or on horseback, with three hours the start of his pursuers, Cuban bloodhounds would have compassed his capture. A sudden, well arranged surprise was the only chance to secure him.

Vasquez' visitors in the Los Angeles jail included numerous ladies, "many," as reporter Beers noted, "belonging to the higher circles of society." As for that, Vasquez probably could not vouch, for he was not too well acquainted with *gringo* society and thus had no way of knowing who belonged to the truly elite. There were, however, several *yanqui* ladies who did come to the jail to talk to Vasquez, all pretending to be calling out of pure humane interest, making certain that he was not being mistreated because of his reputation and the nature of the charges against him. One of them brought a small bouquet of roses from her yard to brighten his cell. The female callers spoke to Vasquez warmly and some of them--one suspects--touched his hand in a more-than-merely-friendly way when the sheriff wasn't looking. In some instances, Vasquez seems to have been given the clear impression that if he were able to cheat the hangman, he would be welcome to visit.

Some newspapers in other parts of the state expressed resentment over the number of visitors--especially the women--who called upon the prisoner in his cell. One incensed editorial writer accused them of "toadying to villainy" and "lionizing Vasquez." The prisoner was in all likelihood amused when he heard that some were outraged. Vasquez no doubt felt it was only proper that he should be treated with the respect due an enemy general who had tried but failed, who nevertheless had fought bravely and well. After all, Vasquez might have argued, if he had been successful in his crusade to retake California in the name of his people, he would have been lionized worldwide for leading a revolution in the name of justice. He may have become another Simón Bolivar.

There were attempts to help Vasquez financially, but not all of them appeared inspired by generosity. *The Evening Express*, *The Star* and *The Herald* all ran an ad that read:

> To the Public--Wounded, a prisoner, and in the shadow of approaching death, or a more to be dreaded incarceration, an unfortunate and sinful man appeals to the charitable among men, of whatever nation, to contribute to a fund to enable him to place his case fairly before the world and the jury to sit in judgment upon him, hereby asserting his innocence of the higher crimes imputed to him, and his ability to establish the fact at a fair and impartial trial.
>
> Tiburcio Vasquez

As Vasquez apparently did not place or give his approval for that ad, it must be concluded that it was the work of some grasping attorney, anxious to get on his case at no financial loss to himself. The bandit disavowed any responsibility for it.

One of the more interesting sidelights of his capture was the production at the Merced Theater in Los Angeles of a burlesque entitled *The Life of Vasquez*. This reportedly intrigued the outlaw, who chatted several times with Samuel Piercy, the actor cast in the title role, so that there would be a more lifelike portrayal. Writer Nadeau claimed that Vasquez loaned his clothes to the actor and even "graciously offered" to play the lead if Sheriff Rowland would give him permission.

The sheriff was not so inclined.

The show, however, went on without Vasquez in person and ran for a full two performances.

On May 22, 1874, the doctor announced that Vasquez had recovered sufficiently to be taken north where hc was to stand trial. Late the next day, wearing the gambler's suit he had been given, he was led from the jail while several hundred onlookers crowded the street. There was some applause, but the level of excitement had subsided somewhat in the week or so that he had been in captivity. Now it was more a matter of curiosity. Perhaps people only wanted to be able to tell their grandchildren they had seen the great Tiburcio Vasquez in person.

Not only were his wrists and ankles secured by chains, he was in the grasp of two deputies while Undersheriff Johnson led the way. He was placed in a wagon and driven to the railroad station, from where he was taken the 20 or so miles to San Pedro. There, they boarded a steamer, the Senator. There were other *gringos* and *Mexicanos* staring as he was taken up the gangway and made to sit in a small cabin while one or the other of the deputies sat watching him carefully the entire time.

After a night and a day of this, they arrived in San Francisco Bay and were soon dockside, where another crowd pressed forward to see the captured Vasquez. Then he was taken in another cart to the local jail where once again he was visited by a parade of newspaper reporters and some local *gringo* politicians anxious to get their names into the newspapers. And, as in Los Angeles, there were numerous women--including some seemingly not unknown in society circles--who came to see him. As usual, he treated them graciously, probably discerning in their eyes and manners a hidden fantasy of riding away with him to the secret canyons and making love under the stars. He might have wondered what they would think if they had known what it was really like to spend a cold night without a campfire for fear of being detected by a posse. Or to sleep among the rocks for weeks at a time, washing in a muddy creek.

One of his visitors in San Francisco was Alameda County Sheriff Harry N. Morse, who came across the bay from Oakland to see the man he had pursued so fruitlessly half the length of the state. Perhaps he only wanted the satisfaction of being certain Vasquez was locked up at last. Morse was ushered into Vasquez' cell wearing a jauntily cocked derby hat and a gray suit with a vest and gold watch chain. Under other circumstances, the bandit would have quickly appropriated the watch. Apparently Morse was curious about Vasquez' published statement that he had always been aware of the sheriff's movements and had been close to his camp on several occasions. Vasquez, who was the epitome of grace now that he was in captivity, probably assured Morse that he had only been trying to make the interview more interesting.

After no more than two or three days in San Francisco, Vasquez was taken by Monterey County Sheriff J.B. Smith and his old enemy, Sheriff Adams of Santa Clara County, to Salinas, where he was jailed to await trial. As there were reports circulating that attempts would be made to take him from the train and lynch him, the officers kept close watch on the crowds that gathered along the way.

There was a great deal being written about Vasquez in the newspapers, including the following by the editor of *The San Jose Mercury*:

> The eminent cutthroat has come and gone. He passed through on the 11:30 train in custody of Sheriff Smith's posse. Perhaps there was not one present but felt that the prisoner was going to certain and merited doom under the law of the land; yet had he by any possibility jumped from that car and escaped, some of them would have cheered him as they would a bad dog set loose with a tin pan tied to his tail.
>
> All of which is consistent with the inconsistency of human nature. As long as Vasquez, the vulgar, ordinary, cowardly highway assassin and robber, was at large, the cry was "Down with him!" but he is no sooner brought down than an exceedingly vulgar sentiment discloses itself, commiserating the robber on account of his insignificant wounds, and "Oh, poor-fellow"-ing him for a sort of 'bloody, bold and resolute' hero of delightful romance. This sentiment will begin to dissipate towards Tres Pinos, where the feeling against the outlaw is intense; and the San Francisco papers affect to know that an attempt to lynch him is not among the improbabilities, by the exasperated friends of the victims of his atrocities.

Although Vasquez would not have totally appreciated the manner in which that was written, he probably would have agreed with some of the conclusions. It was indeed interesting that once he was wounded and in custody, many of those who previously shouted for his capture stood in the street and applauded him as he was led to jail. There were many other stories, of course, including one that ran in *The Post*, termed by Beers "the leading evening journal of the coast." The Post described Vasquez as follows:

> There is nothing particularly ferocious in the appearance of the famous outlaw, and every day in the week there are three times as forbidding-looking fellows in the police docks, charged with petit larceny and assault and battery. He is about medium height, with a wiry, compact, yet slight figure, and does not, probably, weigh more than 145 pounds. His face, once seen, is never forgotten. It is that of a man self-possessed, cool, quiet, and determined, and indicates the stealth of the panther rather than the ferocity of the tiger. In every lineament of his pale, saffron face there is a will strongly marked; and one is impressed with his ability to organize and plan. But there seems to be some requisite wanting in the execution.
>
> The features are quite regular, forehead high and retreating, and head well shaped. His eye is a light gray and deep-set (the left upper eyelid drooping, giving the eye the appearance of being defective), and when speaking of matters that interest him, his whole face lights up with animation and his eye fairly sparkles. The expression of dogged resolution fades away into smiles, and in listening to his peculiarly soft voice one almost forgets the brutal robber and murderer, whose revolting crimes have so shocked the whole state, and made his name a terror in the southern country.

Thus, as he awaited trial, Vasquez was receiving mixed reviews.

Chapter 18
THE VERDICT: DEATH

I am innocent of killing anyone since I was born...

That was Vasquez' testimony. In all the interviews he granted and in all the conversations he had with jailers during the several months between his capture and his trial, he consistently denied having killed any of the three men who died in the raid on Snyder's store at Tres Pinos. His insistence, however, did nothing to ease the feelings against him in San Benito County, which had recently been created by dividing Monterey County and was where the Tres Pinos raid had occurred.

Sheriff Adams and his officers, who accompanied Vasquez on the train from San Francisco to Salinas, where he was to be held pending trial in the San Benito County seat of Hollister, were obviously worried over reports that he was to be lynched the moment he was taken from the train. When they passed through San Jose, a large crowd gathered at the station to gawk. Vasquez was determined to show them he was not afraid. Although it made his guards nervous, he stood straight in the doorway of the mail car that served as his traveling cell. He smiled. He probably would have raised his fist to show the defiance of a revolutionary, but the handcuffs made that awkward. The people stared at him and became strangely quiet, as though they could not believe that he was the monster they had been reading about.

No one tried to lynch him.

He was held at the Salinas jail under heavy guard for a few days, but security there was considered inadequate. The lawmen still remembered what had happened to his friend, Anastacio Garcia, who had been stretched like a strip of jerky. Vigilante committees were not yet a thing of the past. The facilities at Salinas were only slightly safer than those at Hollister, where he was to stand trial. So it was decided to move him to the jail at San Jose, in Santa Clara County.

It was while he was in jail in San Jose that he learned what had happened to Lebrado Corona, who had been captured with him at Greek George's place. Corona had been convicted in Los Angeles for taking part in the Repetto robbery and was sentenced to San Quentin for seven years. No doubt Vasquez thought about the possibility that he might be sent back to that dreadful prison, where he had spent too many years away from the canyons and open sky. He made it clear that he preferred hanging to being locked up for the rest of his life.

In a few days, he was taken to Hollister to be arraigned on the San Benito County indictment for the murder of hotel operator Leander Davidson at Tres Pinos. He could see more anger in the eyes of the *gringos* there, because he was back in the neighborhood of the crime. The atmosphere was heavy with a brooding hatred. There were mutterings about him being a bloodthirsty "greaser" and some brave talk from men who would have been speechless with terror had Vasquez not been handcuffed and marched from the wagon into the small wooden courthouse between two armed deputies.

Because the courtroom was small, spectators were kept out in the dirt street, where they could be heard taunting the prisoner--with more bravado now because Vasquez was not looking at them.

Vasquez wrote a letter to the judge, asking that the trial be moved out of San Benito County. He was not unacquainted with the device of seeking a change of venue. In his flawless penmanship, Vasquez told the judge that "the popular excitement in the county is so great against me as to endanger my personal safety were I to appear in person..." He could not get a fair trial there, he wrote, because "the people of said county en mass are so prejudiced against me...they entertain such ill will towards me..."

And, displaying the writing talent that had attracted praise from his instructor when he was a student in General Castro's school, he declared, "This statement is not the confession of cowardice, but of a conviction that unrestrained public rage has no heart as it has no ears."

The judge was only too willing to send the trial of the dangerous Tiburcio Vasquez someplace else. He probably kept a nervous eye on the closed doorway to make certain the crowd had not yet overpowered the deputies in its eagerness to burst into the courtroom. Too, there were rumors that Vasquez' lieutenant, Cleovaro Chavez, was gathering an army of revolutionaries in the hills and planned to sweep down on the town to rescue their captain. The judge rapped the top of his desk with his gavel and murmured, "So ordered."

So trial was set for Santa Clara County and Vasquez was returned to San Jose jail, where the climate was less threatening, and where he could receive the frequent visitations of newspaper reporters and of ladies anxious to talk to the fabled Vasquez. His cell was constantly the repository for bouquets of flowers lovingly picked by delicate hands, or for one sort of baked confection or another.

He had not been in the San Jose jail more than a short time when Abdon Leiva was brought there to be held pending his appearance as the star witness at Vasquez' trial. Reporter Sawyer asked Vasquez how he felt about his former comrade. Vasquez replied that he bore no ill will toward him. Actually, Vasquez would have shot his former *compadre* cheerfully if he had been able to catch him beyond the view of the jailers. Sawyer, hungry for something dramatic to write about, asked whether Vasquez would like to speak to Leiva. Vasquez did not want the public to see him as anything other than a forgiving, gentle man. He said, "*Por cierto.*" Sheriff Adams then brought Leiva into the cell and Vasquez stood looking at him. Leiva's eyes could not meet those of Vasquez. He stared at the floor. At last, aware that they were being watched closely by the reporter, Vasquez thrust out a hand. After an awkward moment, Leiva took it stiffly, then pulled back as if it held a pistol.

"Do you want to talk to Leiva?" the sheriff asked.

"No," Vasquez said. "I only wanted to see him." His tone was one Leiva could not mistake.

Sheriff Adams then turned to Leiva. "Do you want to say anything to Vasquez?"

"No," Leiva murmured. The sheriff led Leiva away to his own cell. The two never spoke again in each other's presence until the trial.

Rosario came to the jail to see Leiva, perhaps to seek his forgiveness. Hoffer, however, wrote that Rosario wept "and begged him not to testify against Vasquez." But Leiva could not forget how he had been wronged, Hoffer related. "Rosario had her day of love. Now had come his day of revenge." They separated in silence, the author said. Rosario left "like an aged, broken woman. They never met again."

According to Sawyer, Leiva told his wife that as soon as he was released, as the authorities had promised him, he was going to take the children and return to his native Chile, "that he never would have gone with Vasquez but for his wife's importunities." Leiva purportedly believed that Rosario was visiting him only to "pump" him on behalf of Vasquez. "He was on his guard, however, and would not bite," Sawyer wrote.

She never asked to see Vasquez.

Vasquez probably could not understand that. What had happened to the burning love she had professed to have for him? One could not depend upon women to remain faithful. Hoffer's picture hardly fits the Rosario who told *The San Francisco Chronicle* what terrible things Tiburcio Vasquez had done to her. But if Rosario did not drop in on him, Vasquez had plenty of other company. Sawyer wrote that "while the bandit chief was in San Jose, thousands of people visited him." That may have been an exaggeration. At any rate, Sawyer went on:

> He usually sat in his chair with a smile that was childlike and bland, gave a courteous reception to all and seemed to take great delight in his position. His vanity was inordinate, and whenever a young lady (half the visitors were of the weaker sex) would approach near to where he sat, he would appear as pleased as a monkey at the present of a tin trumpet. He evidently regarded himself as a hero, and from the false sympathy he received from a portion of the other sex, it is no wonder that his head got slightly turned.

The reporters who came to see him were only too happy to publish his statements that he did not have funds enough to hire a capable attorney. It was not long before a purse was organized--possibly by one of the charming ladies who chose to remain anonymous--and public contributions began to mount. Before many days had gone by, he found that his benefactors had hired two lawyers to conduct his defense: B.P. Tully and a former San Francisco judge named C.B. Darwin. These two came to see Vasquez, well attended by reporters whom they carefully instructed on the spelling of their names. Tully was from San Benito County and did not seem entirely sure of himself. He informed Vasquez that he had defended Moreno, who was tried several months earlier for the killing of the Portuguese sheepherder at Tres Pinos. As Moreno had been found guilty and hanged, Vasquez could not have found that very comforting.

As the time went by, Vasquez spent countless hours practicing his beautiful handwriting and never wanting for visitors, small gifts and attention by the press. He posed for photographs, one of which was printed up as a souvenir with a biographical sketch of him on the back side. He sold them at 50 cents each, complete with his flowing autograph. There were several court appearances, which always seemed to lead to nothing but postponements for one reason or another, often because his attorneys or the prosecutors were seeking to subpoena new witnesses and needed more time. At last, however, he was to be tried in the Third District Court at San Jose before Judge David Belden. By then, it was Jan. 5, 1875. Vasquez was specifically charged with the murder of Leander Davidson, but not for that of the teamster, Redford, whom he also was believed to have killed.

The defendant was dressed for the occasion in the fine black suit taken from the body of the dead Los Angeles gambler and marched into a courtroom that was crowded with spectators--many of them women. Vasquez was to be prosecuted by a high-powered team, led by no less than state Atty. Gen. John Lord Love. He was assisted by N.C. Briggs and W.E. Lovett of Hollister as well as Dist. Atty. Bodley of Santa Clara County. They sat watching Vasquez enter. Only one of the defense attorneys was there, however. It was Tully. Vasquez appeared to be severely out-numbered. Judge Belden rapped his gavel to call the case: "The people versus Tiburcio Vasquez."

Tully stood and said, "Your Honor, if it please this court, the defense asks for a continuance in the light of an unexpected development."

Judge Belden peered down at Tully and wanted to know, "*What* unexpected development?"

It turned out that Judge Darwin, who was the chief defense attorney, had suddenly decided to withdraw from the case. Tully seemed unable to explain it. He told the judge that late the night before, Darwin had--in Beers' words--"expressed dissatisfaction with some act of the defendant and announced his determination of throwing up the case..." Tully said he thought he had talked Darwin out of quitting, only to learn, just before court opened, "that Mr. Darwin had gone back on the arrangement of the previous evening and had withdrawn as counsel."

That cut little ice with Judge Belden, who noted that the trial had been stalled for four months by one continuance after another and that Tully, being a resident of the county where the crime was committed and having defended Teodoro Moreno, should be able to handle the case. He refused to postone the matter again, but allowed two new attorneys, W.H. Collins and J.A. Moultrie, to assist in defense of the prisoner.

Both Collins and Moultrie were, like the departed Mr. Darwin, former judges who still enjoyed being called "Judge." They showed up at the defense table just about the time the first panel of prospective jurors was seated. Neither of them shook Vasquez' hand or introduced himself, but conducted a quiet conversation with Tully as though the client were not even present. Then they began questioning members of the jury panel. How did they feel about Mexicans? How did they feel about hanging people convicted of murder? Had they ever been robbed by bandits or had any relatives been through such an experience?

As Vasquez listened, he probably felt that the word "Mexican" came out of their mouths like something they did not quite want to talk about. As though they were defending some common thief or holdup man rather than the famous Tiburcio Vasquez, who--but for the bad luck of having a jealous husband turn on him--would have raised an army to retake California.

By noon, only five jurors had been selected. Judge Belden sent for 50 more prospects. Finally, late in the day, a dozen men were in the jury box and the state was ready to go through the formality of a trial. It actually began the morning of January 6 with the galleries, as Beers noted, "filled with ladies representing the elite and respectability of the city." Half of the law enforcement officers of the state were in attendance, too, it seemed. They included Sheriff Billy Rowland from Los Angeles County.

There were numerous reporters from San Jose and San Francisco, one of whom wrote, "Vasquez seemed pleased at the sight of the large crowd in the court room, but his glances were generally unblushingly bestowed upon the ladies in the gallery."

San Benito County Dist. Atty. Briggs told the jury that the prosecution meant to prove that in August of 1873 Tiburcio Vasquez had conspired with Chavez, Moreno, Gonzalez and Leiva to rob Snyder's store at Tres Pinos and that Vasquez himself had killed both Leander Davidson and George Redford. Vasquez had actually been indicted only for the murder of Davidson. Briggs called the first prosecution witness: Abdon Leiva.

Leiva took the stand in his formless jail clothing, never looking at Vasquez. He was questioned through an interpreter and gave short answers in Spanish, sometimes so quietly that he had to be asked to repeat. Vasquez stared at him as he went through the same story he apparently had told at Moreno's trial. Hoffer wrote that Leiva "made Rosario and Vasquez pay for every moment of tenderness and for every kiss." He described the plan to rob Tres Pinos and swore that Vasquez himself killed Davidson and Redford.

When Leiva had finished his testimony, Vasquez' attorney said, "You do not like Tiburcio Vasquez, do you?"

"No," answered Leiva. "There is no injury that I would not do to him."

The prosecutors then produced witnesses to back up Leiva's testimony. These included Santa Clara County Sheriff John H. Adams as well as Andrew Snyder, the store owner, and John Utzerath, his clerk. Also testifying were Snyder's wife and two or three persons who had been in the store at the time as well as D.F.H. McPhail, the man Vasquez had robbed a short distance from the store just before the principal event. All offered damning versions of the famous raid on Snyder's store.

And, there was Rosario.

Whom Vasquez had loved in his fashion and had taken into the hills, in his view sheltering her from all the dangers there. She would not meet Vasquez' eyes as she sat in the witness chair replying in low murmurs to the questions of prosecutor Love. Rosario sat with her head down, looking at her entwined fingers. She appeared to have regained her health; was no longer thin and pale as she had been when Vasquez had last seen her. But she had forgotten her love for him. She said she had heard Vasquez boast of killing Davidson and Redford. She claimed he had abandoned her in the mountains of Southern California, far from home and friends.

When at last she was finished and was allowed to leave the chair, Vasquez may have managed to catch her eye for an instant. One would suppose he smiled, to show her that he held no hard feelings for her; that he understood she was trying to return to the life he had taken her out of. She would have looked away quickly.

In the view of many, the most damaging part of the case against Vasquez was the testimony of McPhail, who had been stopped not far from Snyder's store by Vasquez and Chavez a few minutes before the robbery 18 months earlier. Testifying while Vasquez was out of the courtroom, McPhail said he was positive it was Vasquez he had encountered there and who had allowed him to keep his watch.

Finally, it was Vasquez' turn. His lawyers put him on the stand. After McPhail's testimony, he had decided it was useless to pretend that it was a case of mistaken identity. His only hope lay in convincing the jury that he had not done the shooting. As he stood to be sworn in, his eyes swept the gallery. The women smiled at him, or clasped their hands together. The men stared around at them unhappily. It was a pity from Vasquez' viewpoint that women were not allowed on the jury.

Tully began to question the bandit, allowing him to tell how the raid on Snyder's store had been planned and how he had told his men that "no blood should be shed and no women violated."

Vasquez said that Leiva and Romulo Gonzalez had gone ahead. He claimed the three victims were dead by the time he got there; that he had remonstrated with Leiva and Gonzalez about it. "I did not kill any human beings on that occasion," he testified. "I am innocent of killing anyone since I was born. I did not kill anyone at Tres Pinos. There was no necessity..."

Vasquez could see by the expressions on the faces of the 12 jurymen that they did not believe this. Throughout the gallery, the ladies smiled bravely, doing their best to encourage Vasquez. He adored them all. Watching from the gallery, as she had since the beginning, was Vasquez' sister, Maria Laria.

Finally, his testimony was over. Vasquez marched back to the defense table and sat down.

The next day, "Judge" Collins faced the jurors to make a final appeal on Vasquez' behalf. He ranted on for what seemed like an hour or so, referring to "the roaring river of passion" and the "black clouds of prejudice" that prompted "great damnable cries for revenge coming from a maddened populace." The attorney general, he said, "not content with asking justice at your hands, holds before you a cup and says, 'Fill it with blood, fill it with blood!' "

After drawing upon the Holy Bible for some references that may or may not have applied in Vasquez' case, Collins noted that Vasquez had been "hunted down like a dog" and that although District Attorney Briggs was "fully competent...the principal law officer of the state comes here to add the weight of his great abilities to the prosecution."

Collins also took the occasion to note that Leiva, the main witness against Vasquez, was a murderer and a traitor. "Gentlemen of the jury," Collins said, "I commit to your keeping the life and liberty of Tiburcio Vasquez."

He sat down, looking at Vasquez for one of the few times in the trial. Vasquez gathered he was expecting approval. But it had not been the speech of a man convinced his client was innocent. Vasquez turned his gaze back to the women. They, at least, were on his side.

Then Atty. Gen. Love--who apparently saw this trial as a stepping stone to the governorship--got up to demand a first-degree murder verdict and the death penalty. "Unless the law is vindicated," he said angrily, "all the great rights and benefits of humanity become impossible, and life itself is an empty vanity. 'He who is merciful to the bad is cruel to the good.' All that the state asks is justice. If you believe he is wrongfully accused, for God's sake, let him go. But if you believe he is guilty, punish him, so that others may be deterred from following his example."

That brought applause from the men in the audience. The evidence, Love insisted, had shown that "the little man with the black cloak" was Vasquez and that he was the one who had shot Davidson.

When Judge Belden gave his charge to the jury, he made clear that under the law it did not matter whether Vasquez had fired the shot that killed Davidson. It was, he said, "not necessary for the prosecution to show that the defendant fired the fatal shot, or by whom it was fired. It is sufficient if it was fired by one of the members of the party there associated together for and actually engaged in robbery and that it was fired in furtherance of the common pupose to commit this robbery, that in such a case all of the persons thus associated in the robbery are equally accountable for the homicide,. and all thus associating and acting, are guilty of murder in the first degree."

Vasquez could hear the rope creaking.

At last, the jurors retired to make their decision. There were rumors of an attempt by some San Benito County *Americanos* to seize Vasquez in open court and lynch him in case the jury did not order him hanged by the state.

It was not until 7 o'clock in the evening that the jury came back. The courtroom was as crowded as it had been throughout the testimony. According to Beers, "nine-tenths of the occupants of the gallery were ladies." Beers wrote that Vasquez' face "wore a deadly pallor, and he glanced nervously from right to left as if expecting to see the frightful gibbet, with all its ghastly belongings."

The courtroom fell silent as the jurymen filed into their box. The foreman handed a slip of paper to the clerk, who read the verdict: "We, the jury, find the defendant guilty of murder in the first degree, and assign the death penalty."

There was applause from the *gringo* men in gallery. The women, it was reported in the press, wept. Some of them fainted.

Tiburcio Vasquez, who may or may not have recaptured California from the invaders if he had not been caught, was to die.

Chapter 19
ADIÓS, TIBURCIO

Pronto.

The number of women who desired to visit Vasquez in his cell increased remarkably after the jury found him guilty. Several of them appear to have suggested quietly that if he could persuade the sheriff to accommodate them with a private room for a short while he could taste paradise before being dispatched to hell by the hangman. Vasquez apparently declined with thanks. Somehow, he seemed to have lost his desire for such things. Perhaps the fire in his loins had been dampened by the realization that it was a hunger for women that had led him to the steps of the gallows in the first place.

Sweet, faithless Rosario.

On Jan. 23, 1875, two weeks from the day the verdict had come in, Judge Belden formally pronounced sentence, ordering that Vasquez should be hanged in the San Jose jail yard. Beers wrote that Tiburcio accepted the sentencing without any show of emotion, because "he was either possessed of an inhuman or unnatural heart, so that he had no care even for himself, or had the most absolute control of his nerves."

The judge made it clear he felt he was sending to his death a common highwayman, not a revolutionary hero. "This life you have led," he said, "soon to be ended, is full of admonition to those who give heed to the transgressor. It points to a life of crime, of violence, and outlawry, with its fit ending in a death of shame. Well may those who are following in the footsteps of your earlier years take warning from your fate, and turn while they may, from the path that leads to certain destruction."

Vasquez may have considered leaping to his feet to inform the judge that the only shame was on the part of the *gringos* who had invaded California to rape both its land and its women. But he kept his peace. The judge was becoming more enthusiastic about his own words: "The motive of your life, as shown by the criminal records of the state, disclosed by your associates and told by yourself, is one unbroken record of lawlessness and outrage..."

Outrage? Vasquez could tell him about outrage; about drunken *gringo soldados* and miners, or about vigilantes hanging *Mexicanos* for little or no reason.

The judge noted that Vasquez had "entered upon manhood a convicted felon in the penitentiary of the state" and observed that "the sharp admonition of this early punishment was wholly lost upon you..." Once out of prison, the judge said, Vasquez had "adopted the life of a robber, and entered upon a career of outrage, pillage and murder, with neither limit nor interruption until the strong hand of the law reached forth and grappled you."

His Honor was just getting warmed up. For years, he said, in the section of the state "plagued" by Vasquez' presence, "outrages known to be yours, crimes self-aroused, made your name the synonym for all that was wicked and infamous..."

And, he suggested, Vasquez had probably done a lot of other things that people hadn't heard about. "What hidden crimes, what secret deeds of violence, unseen and unrecognized by men, may stain your hands and burden your conscience, yourself can alone know," he said.

By the time he got around to Snyder's store, the judge was in full cry:

"It appears that you planned the robbery of the store at Tres Pinos, and with a band of kindred spirits, armed and prepared for murder as well as for pillage, you attacked the place you proposed plundering. Your number, your preparation and the completeness of your surprise made resistance hopeless, and it was not even attempted; and without bloodshed and opposition you might have secured you booty and made your escape.

"This did not content you. The men you slew were not those whose goods you coveted. Two of them were strangers and wayfarers that an unhappy chance threw in your cruel way. They possessed nothing you could desire. They made no obstacle to your purpose. Helpless, unarmed, and unresisting, you slew them in the mere wantonness of butchery, and with the corpses at your feet, you gathered the paltry spoils of your four-fold crime and fled to the mountains..."

The speech Judge Belden had prepared for the moment was much longer and filled with the kind of righteous indignation he probably felt would land him in all thc *yanqui* newspapers. He was, of course, correct in that regard. It is enough to report that he concluded by saying:

"The judgment is death. That you be taken hence and securely kept by the sheriff of Santa Clara County, until Friday, the 19th day of March, 1875. That upon that day, between the hours of 9 o'clock in the morning and four in the afternoon, you be by him hanged by the neck until you are dead. And may the Lord have mercy on your soul."

Having had his say, the judge looked toward the reporters to make certain they had got down the gist of it, swept a disapproving eye across the ladies in the gallery who were touching handkerchiefs to their eyes and making little moans of distress, then rose and marched from the courtroom.

Not once did he glance at Vasquez.

Vasquez' attorneys, having been turned down by the judge on their appeal of the verdict, now petitioned the state Supreme Court for a new trial, but even their client knew there was no hope there. All the members of the court were *gringos*.

Shortly after the sentencing, a great deal of excitement was generated by the discovery of a letter that had been dropped into a Wells Fargo box in Hollister. It bore the name of Vasquez' lieutenant, Cleovaro Chavez. It was in Spanish and it read:

> NOTICE TO THE TOWN OF HOLLISTER:
>
> Know you, that in regard to the acts committed by the captain of my company, I say that, finding myself guilty of those acts, I flew to Mexico; but having been informed while there that Vasquez was under sentence of death, I have returned as far as this place with the aim of disclosing the falseness of the evidence sworn against him, and in case Vasquez should be hanged, to quickly mete out a recompense.

Whether Chavez had actually written it was questionable, for it did not sound like him. The *Americanos* were rather worked up about it for a while, though. Some were certain that Vasquez had caused the letter to be written and others just as sure that a small army of his men were about to ride down out of the hills.

The letter went on:

> I let you know that if Vasquez is hung by his enemies, who, through fear, have turned against him, I will show you I know how to avenge the death of my captain.

The letter writer added that Chavez and Abdon Leiva had disregarded Vasquez' orders at Tres Pinos, declaring, "It was I subsequently who was at the head of the affair at Tres Pinos, in which the murders were committed."

It was never learned who actually wrote it.

Vasquez' death sentence was not overturned and March 19 was rapidly approaching. As Beers noted in his book, Vasquez "was visited by hundreds every week, many of his visitors being ladies and gentlemen of the highest respectability, who called not to 'lionize' the outlaw, but to gratify a natural desire to see and converse with the man or monster about whom so much had been said and written."

A reporter from *The San Jose Patriot* interviewed him and wrote that he found Vasquez "cheerful in conversation as usual, and in appearance looking as well as at any time during the confinement."

There was no American Civil Liberties Union to come to the aid of Vasquez. There would be no years of waiting on Death Row while appeals went on and on before one court and then another. On March 12, the state Supreme Court turned down the petition by his attorney. Sheriff Adams began to prepare for the big day. He obtained from Sacramento the same gallows that had been used to hang Charles Mortimer, a robber and murderer, as well as two or three others who had never attained the fame achieved by Tiburcio Vasquez. The latter no doubt felt that Adams should have had a special gallows built for him.

There was one small attempt to have the execution postponed for a while. Remarkably, the request came from Los Angeles County Sheriff Billy Rowland and some other prominent citizens in that area, who sent a telegram to the governor suggesting that hanging Vasquez was apt to stir up trouble and that some "innocent persons" might get hurt.

The governor, however, said he saw no reason to put it off.

With that last small hope gone, Vasquez told the press that he was ready to die "as a man and a Californian."

Two nights before Vasquez was to hang, Sheriff Adams, Undersheriff Winchell and reporter Beers spent several hours talking to him in his cell. He told them, "I assert as a dying man that the man found dead near the door of Snyder's store was killed by Abdon Leiva. The two others were killed by Gonzalez, now supposed to be in Mexico."

Obviously, Vasquez did not feel compelled to suddenly break down and confess. No doubt he wanted the *gringos* of California to spend a few years wondering whether, in fact, they had hanged an innocent man. He could only hope it would make them feel to some extent their own guilt over what they had done to the *Mexicanos* in California.

It was Winchell--the undersheriff who was reported to have been less than heroic on the day that Harry Morse killed Vasquez' old friend Juan Soto in their famed duel--who then asked the doomed bandit what he thought about the possibility of life in the beyond. Winchell said, "I believe implicitly in a future state of existence--in the immortality of the soul. What is your belief on that point?"

Vasquez replied that he did not know, but added, "I hope your belief is correct, for in that case I shall see my old sweethearts together on Friday."

Given the inclination of former lady friends to display hostility, it was questionable whether that was actually a pleasant prospect.

By this time Vasquez and his visitors had been joined by one of his lawyers, Judge Collins, and two or three of Adams' deputies. Beers then asked Vasquez whether he had any last words for the people. Vasquez could not allow an opportunity like that to pass. He dictated his message of regret in Spanish to a deputy named Selman. Beers later printed the rather awkward English version in his newspaper and in his book about Vasquez.

"To the fathers and mothers of children:

"Standing upon the portals of the unknown and unknowable world, and looking back upon the life of this, as I have seen, I would urge upon you to make it your greatest aim here to so train, instruct and govern the young to whom you have given life that they be kept aloof as far as is the nature of things possible, from the degrading companionship of the immoral and vicious.

"The general welfare of society depends upon the strict performance on your part of this duty. The state of society in the next generation depends upon the manner in which the children of the present are instructed and trained.

"I wish the children throughout the world, who may read the incidents of my life, to take warning in time of the example before them of me, and to realize the force of the saying, 'The way of the transgressor is hard'--the truth of which is now being verified to me.

"The world must not be allowed to think by anything I have here said that I have intended to reflect upon the instruction and training I received from my own parents. I affirm they did all they could to bring me up the right way. Circumstances which they could not control threw me among the vicious, and I disobeyed their wise teachings.

"I hereby ask pardon from each and everyone whom I have in any way injured; asking that pardon with all the earnestness that only a dying man can; asking also the prayers of all good Christian people that forgiveness may be extended to, not only by those that I have wronged, but by the Great Father whose laws I have so ruthlessly trampled upon. The forgiveness that

I have asked from those whom I have wronged, I freely and completely give to all who have injured me.

"I thank my counsel, and each of them, for their devotion to me in my hour of distress. I express my gratitude to Sheriff Adams, Undersheriff Winchell and Deputies Selman and Curtis, for their great kindness to me during the period I have been in their custody. I thank my brothers for their brotherly love extended to me during all the time of my troubles, and to my darling and devoted sister I render inexpressible thanks.

"Oh, sister of mine, thy love to me will buoy me up in my last moments!

"I commit my soul and the hereafter that is before me to the keeping of the Maker, without whose help I can never expect a complete pardon.

"Farewell, brothers! Farewell, sisters, dear! The end has come!"

The sister singled out by Vasquez for special mention clearly was Maria, who reportedly attended the trial every day.

The bandit chief probably could see that his *gringo* jailers and the reporter did not know enough Spanish to understand quite what he had said. Vasquez would be in his grave before they realized how moving and sentimental he had become in his final hours. No doubt he was rather proud of his words, although one suspects that most of them were a bit insincere.

Still, the *Americanos* were not satisfied. Sheriff Adams suggested it might be a good idea for Vasquez to leave some word for his men, so that they would not rise up and cause trouble for the law once their captain was dead. Again, Vasquez obliged, dictating:

"To my former associates--I wish you, who will doubtless expect to hear some last word of farewell from me, whose fortunes and adventures you have shared, to ponder well the few words I now deem it proper to say to you. You must well know that I, who could, had I been so disposed, have disclosed to the authorities and to the world the perpetrators of many atrocious crimes, might thus have saved my own life. So you can see, if the world cannot, that to a certain extend this expiation is on my part voluntary. I wish you especially to understand that while I deny having committed the immediate crime of which I have been convicted, and for which I am to suffer death, or of having at any time shed human blood, or taken the life of my fellow man, common sense compels me to realize the justness of the law which holds me responsible for the innocent lives lost in the prosecution of my unlawful calling of robbery. The threats of revenge, which I hear have been made by some of you--threats to retaliate by outrages on the community at large, and by the assassination of my captors, the jury who convicted me, or the officers who have held me a prisoner, are foolish and wrong--for all these people have merely represented the law, and have only acted in the interests of society. By the course threatened you could do me no earthly good, but only bring yourselves in the end to my own fate. Take warning, then, by my fate, and change your course of life while you may.

"I, Tiburcio Vasquez, now about to pay the penalty of a misdirected life, say this to you, my former companions, with the solemn earnestness of a dying man."

Early the next morning, workers began assembling the hand-me-down gallows out in the southwest corner of the jail yard.

Vasquez could see them from the barred window of his cell and could hear the hammers throughout the day. The sound must have been nerve-wracking. An army of people came around the jail to watch the terrible thing erected. At least, Vasquez could see, the *gringos* were going to more trouble for him than they had for Anastacio Garcia, whom they had simply hanged from a beam.

At midmorning, Judge Collins came to see Vasquez, as did Deputy Selman, who read back to the prisoner the English translation of the two statements he had dictated, so that he might make whatever changes he wished. Beers wrote that Vasquez showed some emotion when he listened to the words, "farewell, sisters dear." But he did not allow the *gringos* to see him weep.

Vasquez' sister Maria--now *Señora* Laria--came to see him, along with his brother Francisco of Elizabeth Lake. There were some other relatives with them.

The hanging of Vasquez was to be a major social event. Sheriff Adams even issued formal invitation cards, as though he were putting on a party. The invitations were marked "not transferable."

There were rumors that armed groups of *Mexicanos* were planning to attack San Jose to prevent the execution. There was nothing to these reports, but the deputies were edgy.

At Vasquez' request, the undertakers brought to the jail the coffin his friends had ordered for him. He wished to see it. He gazed at the satin lining, felt the cushions and was satisfied. "I can sleep here forever very well," He said.

He was brought a suit to wear for the hanging, probably so the sheriff would not be embarrassed. The *pantalones* were a little tight, but it did not matter. Vasquez would not be wearing them much. A photographer fussed around for a long time making a portrait of him for the history books.

Finally, on the last night of his life, Vasquez sat smoking a cigar and talking for a while with his guards. Then he fell into a sound sleep. What was done was done. There was nothing he could change now.

Beers wrote:

> Vasquez' last morning on earth found him as imperturbable and cheerful as ever. He arose early, dressed himself tidily for the solemn event so near at hand, and ate a substantial breakfast. At eight o'clock his relatives and friends came to pay their last visit, most of them remaining until nearly noon.

The big event was scheduled for 1:30 P.M. At least two hours before that, the crowd began to gather outside the fence, waiting for admittance to the jail yard. Judge Collins came to see his client again. Why, Vasquez did not know. There was nothing further the man could do for him. The local priest, Father Serda, called on Vasquez about an hour and a half before the appointed hour, promising him that he would find peace in heaven. Vasquez must have had his doubts about that. Certainly he knew he would find no stage coaches to ambush and no Wells Fargo boxes to pry open--wherever he went.

Then a small army of reporters and officials of one kind or another were allowed in while Undersheriff Winchell read to Vasquez the death warrant, which was translated in Spanish line by line. Finally, Sheriff Adams said, "Vasquez, the time has come to march to the scaffold."

"All right," Vasquez agreed, shaking hands all around and giving each person a quick little bow. "*Adiós.*"

With Winchell and Deputy Selman leading the way, Vasquez was taken out into the jail yard. It was an impressive procession made up of Sheriff Adams, Father Serda and numerous newspaper reporters. The place was so packed with spectators that the official party had to force its way through to the wooden gallows. Vasquez climbed the steps and looked down at the sea of expectant *gringo* faces. He offered them a smile. Then, while the priest administered the last rites, he held a small crucifix that Maria had given him. Among those on the scaffold were a few of the lawmen who had hunted him through the mountains and canyons--Sheriff Harry Morse of Alameda County in particular.

When the priest was through, Vasquez took off his coat and handed it to Winchell. Calmly, Vasquez removed his collar to bare his neck for the rope. He could hear the murmur that swept through the crowd. The deputies then strapped his arms to his sides and belted his legs together at the knees and ankles. Winchell placed the noose over his head and around his neck. Vasquez could smell the rope as it came down across his face. The knot was slipped tightly in under his left ear.

Vasquez looked at Winchell.

"*Pronto!*" the condemned man said.

It was the last word of his life.

Bibliography

Bad Company, Joseph Henry Jackson; Harcourt, Brace, New York, 1939.

The California Outlaw, Tiburcio Vasquez, Robert Greenwood; Arno Press, New York, 1947.

The Capture of Tiburcio Vasquez, Los Angeles Times; July 24, 1949.

Crimes and Career of Tiburcio Vasquez, Evening free Lance, Hollister, Calif., 1927.

Dictionary of Mexican-American History, Matt S. Meier and Feliciano Rivera; Greenwood Press, Westport, Conn., 1981.

Fallen Angels, Marvin J. Wolf and Katherine Mader; Facts on File Publications, New York, 1986.

Graphic Description of West Coast Outlaws, Charles Howard Shinn; written for Hubert H. Bancroft in 1888, reprinted by Westernlore Press, Los Angeles, Calif., 1958.

Haunts and Hideouts of Tiburcio Vasquez, Will H. Thrall; manuscript in Huntington Library collection, San Marino, Calif.

History of California, 1848-1859, Vol. VI, Hubert H. Bancroft; The History Company, San Francisco; 1888.

History of Los Angeles, City and County California, compiled by William A. Spalding; J. R. Finnell & Sons, Los Angeles, Calif., circa 1930.

Life, Adventures and Capture of Tiburcio Vasquez, Ben C. Truman; Los Angeles Star, Los Angeles, Calif., 1974.

The Life and Adventures of Joaquin Murrieta, John Rollin Ridge (Yellowbird); W. B. Cooke, 1854; University of Oklahoma Press, Norman, Okla., 1955 edition.

The Life and Career of Tiburcio Vasquez, Eugene Sawyer; Biobooks, Oakland, Calif., 1944. (Written in 1875.)

Recollections of the Vasquez Raid on Snyder's Store in Tres Pinos, Andrew Snyder; manuscript in the Thrall collection, Huntington Library, San Marino, Calif.

The Salinas, Upside-Down River, Anne B. Fisher; Farrar & Rinehart; New York, 1945.

Spanish-Mexican Families of Early California, Marie E. Northrup; Southern California Genealogical Society; Burbank, Calif., 1948.

Tiburcio Vasquez, Ernest R. May; Historical Society of Southern California Quarterly, Vol. 29, 1947.

Tiburcio Vasquez, Bandit, Dominga L. Cervantes; Historic Memories Press, Puyallup, Wash., 1947.

Vasquez, or the Hunted Bandits of the San Joaquin, George A. Beers; Robert M. De Witt, pub: New York, 1875.

West of the West, Robert Kirsch and William S. Murphy; Dutton, New York, 1939.

About the Author

Jack Jones is a retired newspaperman who lives in California with his wife, Brie. He has published four novels: *Journey Into Death, The Animal, Baja* and *Barker Bites Back*, as well as numerous magazine short stories under the pseudonym Jay Edmond.